3001
ESSENTIAL WORDS
FOR A PERFECT
VOCABULARY

Fred N. Grayson

With an introduction by
Prescott Evarts, Jr., Ph.D.
Chairman, Department of English
Associate Professor of English
Monmouth College West
Long Branch, New Jersey

A NAUTILUS COMMUNICATIONS BOOK

ARCO PUBLISHING, INC.
NEW YORK

Published by Arco Publishing, Inc.
215 Park Avenue South, New York, N.Y. 10003

Copyright © 1983 by Nautilus Communications, Inc.

Library of Congress Cataloging in Publication Data

Grayson, Fred N.
3001 essential words for a perfect vocabulary.

"A Nautilus communications book."
1. Vocabulary. 2. English language—Glossaries,
vocabularies, etc. I. Title. II. Title: Three thousand
and one essential words for a perfect vocabulary.
III. Title: Three thousand one essential words for a
perfect vocabulary.
PE1449.G65   1983   428.1   83-8759
ISBN 0-668-05657-6

Printed in the United States of America

INTRODUCTION

"I don't know what you mean by 'glory,'" Alice said.

Humpty Dumpty smiled contemptuously. "Of course you don't—till I tell you. I meant 'there's a nice knock-down argument for you!'"

"But 'glory' doesn't mean 'a nice knock-down argument,'" Alice objected.

"When I use a word," Humpty Dumpty said, in rather a scornful tone, "it means just what I choose it to mean—neither more nor less."

"The question is," said Alice, "whether you can make words mean so many different things."

"The question is," said Humpty Dumpty, "which is to be master—that's all."

Lewis Carroll
Through The Looking Glass

Humpty Dumpty's position is evidently quite defensible among the logicians, but not, unfortunately, in the world. We are quite aware of our present need to improve written and spoken English, and we try to repress the Humpty Dumpty within us, especially when it comes to words.

Using words precisely clarifies a thought, makes a letter convincing, impresses a listener. We must be familiar with the meaning of a word before that word comes naturally to our tongues or pens. If we have the slightest doubt that we may not know the meaning of a word, we should look it up immediately. This book of 3001 essential words is a handy book for just this need—immediate reference at the desk, console, or work table.

Writing is hard work, and we tend to be lazy about looking up words. We say to ourselves that the sentence sounds correct, the spelling seems all right, and chances are the receiver at the other end of the line (the reader) won't catch our error anyway—a dangerous assumption. The receiver at the other end of the line may be a boss or a jealous friend who might like nothing better than to catch us with the wrong word or an incorrect spelling.

There is a certain gloating for people in saying, "Edward never could spell *existence*" or "June will never be able to distinguish between *effect* and *affect*." We should do everything in our power to avoid such criticism, especially since we have become so conscious of good English.

The first step to remedy our laziness is to have a reference book handy at all times. The advantage of this book is its size and convenience; it can fit anywhere without cluttering or getting in the way. It will also be a time-saver, and you will be able to use this book instead of a bulky dictionary.

The second step is to become more closely attuned to the signals in our own mind. If we feel the slightest uneasiness with a word, we should pay attention. Our unconscious may be telling us that we have a mistake in front of us that our conscious mind has not picked up. Then we should look up the word. It is important to get in the habit of looking up a word even if we are sure we know the meaning. We may be surprised to find that we have misused the words for years. It is better to look up words than to trust in our own habitual usage.

The third step (or state of mind) is not to be frustrated by lack of retention. You should look up the word again and again until you have mastered it. This seems odd, but the mind plays tricks all the time. Some big words will be retained immediately—spelling, meaning, and all; other, simpler words might cause us problems for a long time. The mind will continually forget how to spell a word, for it is often confused by similarities in sound.

For instance, people often misspell *grammar* because they confuse it with *hammer*; *existence* may be misspelled as *existance* because of words like *distance* that sound nearly the same. These confusions can be sorted out by constant referral to a reference book. We should never become discouraged because that will accomplish nothing more than laziness; the mistakes will remain uncorrected.

We often misuse words that are close in meaning because we have not taken the time to think them out. A classic example is the difference between *infer* and *imply*. We *infer* or come to a conclusion about something from the evidence offered by someone else. We *imply* or give an impression to someone else by offering them evidence. The two words depict exactly opposite actions, messages being carried in opposite directions.

A fourth step or word of advice has to do with the process of enlarging one's vocabulary. This often brings to mind a crash course, lists of words, definitions hurriedly learned, numerous multiple-choice tests. Such an effort may well be counter-productive and leads more readily to the kinds of confusion that have caused the trouble in the first place. The best way to enlarge a working vocabulary is slowly, a word at a time.

Part of the effort may be to retrieve, from a kind of limbo, words that we read and understand (or think we understand) but do not use naturally. To use a word in speech or even in our own writing is to be familiar with it. We become "familiar" with a word by being sure of its meaning, by looking it up in our reference book.

You should also remember that an enormous vocabulary must also be a useful one. The best writers do not employ overwhelming numbers of learned words to impress us, but use the exact and often the simplest word to enlighten us.

If you are persistent and confident, you will gradually enlarge your useful vocabulary, and there is pleasure in this. There is pleasure in knowing for its own sake; there is pleasure in realizing the practical advantages of increased word power in our business and personal relations.

Prescott Evarts

A

abacus n ab-a-cus: instrument for performing computations
The *abacus* is still widely used in Japan for computation.
abalone n ab-a-lo-ne: an edible mollusk
Some South Sea Islanders subsist on *abalone*.
abandon v a-ban-don: to desert
The dog was *abandoned* by its owner.
abandon n a-ban-don: unrestrained activity
She danced with *abandon* in front of the audience.
abase v a-base: to humiliate
She *abased* him in front of his friends.
abash v a-bash: to embarrass
She was *abashed* at her own behavior.
abate v a-bate: to reduce in intensity or number
The tempest *abates* in fury.
abdicate v ab-di-cate: resign, relinquish formally
The King was forced to *abdicate* when he married a commoner.
abdomen n ab-do-men: stomach area
He had a severe pain in his *abdomen*.
abduct v ab-duct: to kidnap
He was *abducted* by the masked intruders.
aberration n ab-er-ra-tion: a deviation from the right or normal
Many hospital patients suffer from mental *aberration*.
abet v a-bet: to encourage the commission of an offense
Aiding and *abetting* an enemy of the country constitutes treason.
abeyance n a-bey-ance: temporary suspension of action
The strike motion was held in *abeyance* pending contract negotiations.
abhor v ab-hor: to hate
I really *abhor* musical plays.
abject adj ab-ject: miserable, wretched
Many Asians live in a state of *abject* poverty.
abjure v ab-jure: to renounce under oath
A new citizen must *abjure* allegiance to his former country.
ablution n ab-lu-tion: a washing or cleansing
Ablutions are a part of many religious rites.
abnegate v ab-ne-gate: to deny or renounce
He must *abnegate* all his former friends.

abnormal adj ab-nor-mal: unusual, irregular
The *abnormal* way in which he behaved bothered his parents.
abode n a-bode: residence
He moved his *abode* to the other part of town.
abolish v a-bol-ish: to put an end to
They tried to *abolish* the long lunch hour.
abominate v a-bom-i-nate: to hate
I *abominate* having to eat celery.
abortive adj a-bor-tive: ineffectual, unsuccessful
They made an *abortive* attempt to capture the radio station.
abrade v a-brade: to rub off, wear away by friction
Sandpaper is used to *abrade* a rough surface.
abridge v a-bridge: to shorten
The book was *abridged* and did not contain all the information.
abrogate v ab-ro-gate: to annul or abolish
Congress has the right to *abrogate* laws with the consent of the chief
executive.
abrupt adj a-brupt: sudden, quick
He made an *abrupt* departure from the party.
abscond v ab-scond: to steal off to avoid some penalty
The teller *absconded* with the bank's funds.
absolve v ab-solve: to forgive
She was *absolved* by her father.
abstain v ab-stain: to refrain voluntarily from some act
Alcoholics must *abstain* from any indulgence in alcoholic drinks.
abstemious adj ab-ste-mi-ous: moderate in eating and drinking
The *abstemious* eater is seldom overweight.
abstruse adj ab-struse: hard to understand, abstract
The *abstruse* style of the artist confused the viewer.
absurd adj ab-surd: ridiculous
He wore an *absurd* jacket to the party.
abundant adj a-bun-dant: more than enough
There were *abundant* baskets of fruit for the guests.
abusive adj a-bu-sive: insulting, attacking
His language was *abusive* and he was asked to leave.
abut v a-but: to touch, as bordering property
When estates *abut*, borders must be defined properly.
abyss n a-byss: bottomless pit
The *abyss* was deep and treacherous.
accede v ac-cede: to give in to, agree
I will *accede* to your wishes if you cooperate.
access n admission: ac-cess
He received *access* to the files from his boss.

acclaim v ac-claim: to approve, applaud
He *acclaimed* their new production.

acclaim n ac-claim: loud approval
The audience's *acclaim* was overwhelming.

acclimate v ac-cli-mate: accustom to a new enviroment
Visitors to the desert have a hard time *acclimating* themselves to the variations in temperature.

acclivity n ac-cliv-i-ty: upward slope
He viewed the great *acclivity* with dismay as their car chugged along.

accolade n ac-co-lade: an award or praise
He accepted the *accolade* modestly.

accomplice n ac-com-plice: a partner
They were *accomplices* in the crime.

accord n ac-cord: an agreement
All of the members of the council signed the latest *accord*.

accost v ac-cost: to greet, aggressively
The boy was *accosted* by a beggar on the country road.

accouchement n ac-couche-ment: confinement for childbirth
They waited impatiently during her *accouchement*.

accumulate v ac-cu-mu-late: to collect, gather
He *accumulated* a large assortment of stamps.

acerbity n a-cer-bi-ty: bitterness, sourness
The *acerbity* of her wit won her many enemies.

acme n ac-me: highest point
The *acme* of the skyline was the radio tower.

acolyte n ac-o-lyte: an assistant, especially in a religious rite
The youth was anxious to serve as *acolyte* to a priest.

aconite n ac-o-nite: a type of poisonous plant
The *aconites* include wolfsbane and monkshood, which figure in many mystery stories.

acoustic adj a-cous-tic: pertaining to hearing
The *acoustic* qualities of a room may be improved by insulation.

acquiesce v ac-qui-esce: agree, submit
He was forced to *acquiesce* to his boss's demands.

acquit v ac-quit: to declare innocent
The jury voted to *acquit* the defendant.

acrid adj ac-rid: sharp, bitter
The drink left an *acrid* taste in his mouth.

acrimony n ac-ri-mo-ny: harsh or biting language or temper
His *acrimony* resulted from years of disappointment.

acronym n ac-ro-nym: word formed from initials
Radar is an *acronym* for radio detecting and ranging.

actuary n ac-tu-ar-y: an expert who calculates insurance risks

The *actuary* plays an important part in establishing insurance premium rates.

actuate v ac-tu-ate: to put into action, incite
The machine was *actuated* by an electric starter.

acumen n a-cu-men: sharpness, insight
His financial *acumen* helped make him rich.

adage n ad-age: a proverb, a saying that has been in long use
"A stitch in time saves nine" is an old *adage*.

adamant adj ad-a-mant: inflexible, hard
A man must be *adamant* in his determination to succeed.

adapt v a-dapt: to change
He was able to *adapt* himself to the warmer climate.

adduce v ad-duce: to bring forward as a reason or example
In their defense they *adduced* several justifications for their actions.

adept adj a-dept: highly skilled
She was *adept* at skiing.

adept n a-dept: an expert, one who is skilled
He was considered an *adept* in their field of art.

adequate adj ad-e-quate: sufficient
The drink was *adequate* and quenched his thirst.

adhere v ad-here: stick to
He tried to *adhere* the poster to the wall with glue.

adipose adj ad-i-pose: fatty
The doctor removed the *adipose* tissue from around the heart.

adjacent adj ad-ja-cent: along side of, near to
She lived in the *adjacent* building.

adjourn v ad-journ: to postpone, discontinue
They were unable to *adjourn* the meeting for him.

adjunct n ad-junct: something added to
The building was an *adjunct* to the school.

adjure v ad-jure: to charge or command solemnly
The witness was *adjured* to weigh his words carefully.

admonish v ad-mon-ish: to warn
The child was *admonished* by the man and told not to mistreat the dog.

adroit adj a-droit: skillful
The child's *adroit* piano playing made the audience cheer.

adulation n ad-u-la-tion: extreme praise
The movie star was not used to his fans' *adulation*.

advent n ad-vent: arrival
With the *advent* of winter, I start to wear mittens.

adverse adj ad-verse: unfavorable
The movie received *adverse* comments in the papers.

advocate v ad-vo-cate: to speak or write in support of
They tried to *advocate* a new rule in the Congress.

advocate n ad-vo-cate: one who pleads in support of something
He was an *advocate* of free speech.

aesthetic adj aes-thet-ic: pertaining to the beautiful
Modern design seeks to produce machines which have *aesthetic* as well as functional appeal.

affable adj af-fa-ble: sociable, courteous
The dog was *affable* and liked by the neighbors.

affidavit n af-fi-da-vit: a sworn statement in writing
An *affidavit* may serve in place of a personal appearance.

affiliate v af-fil-i-ate: to connect with, to join
He planned to *affiliate* himself with the other team.

affiliate n af-fil-i-ate: one who belongs
He was elected an *affiliate* of the firm.

affinity n af-fin-i-ty: attraction
He had an overpowering *affinity* for chocolate.

affirmation n af-fir-ma-tion: solemn avowal
Quakers and others may testify in court on *affirmation*.

affirmative adj af-fir-ma-tive: agreeing
He was *affirmative* in his decisions.

affirmative n af-fir-ma-tive: an experession of agreement
I will vote in the *affirmative* for that measure.

affluence n af-flu-ence: wealth
They had achieved their *affluence* by hard work.

affluent adj af-flu-ent: abundant, wealthy
The United States is an *affluent* nation.

affront v af-front: to insult
He *affronted* the girl by slamming the door.

affront n af-front: a deliberate insult
The way he acted was an *affront* to his father.

agenda n a-gen-da: schedule of events, list
His talk was to be the first on the *agenda*.

agglomerate v ag-glom-er-ate: to gather into one mass
It was necessasry to *agglomerate* all the minerals into one product to produce the necessary weight.

aggravate v ag-gra-vate: to annoy
His leg *aggravated* him throughout the race.

aggregate v ag-gre-gate: to collect
He was able to *aggregate* a large collection of art.

aggregate n ag-gre-gate: a total
The *aggregate* of all his holdings was immense.

aggressive adj ag-gres-sive: quarrelsome, forward
The child was too *aggressive* to play with the others.
aghast adj a-ghast: frightened, surprised
She was *aghast* at her child's behavior.
agile adj ag-ile: nimble
The child was *agile* climbing the bars.
agitate v ag-i-tate: to disturb; shake
The washing machine *agitated* the clothing in the final cycle.
agnostic n ag-nos-tic: skeptic
He was an *agnostic* when it came to believing in God.
agony n ag-o-ny: great suffering, pain
He was in *agony* after the accident.
agrarian adj a-grar-i-an: having to do with land
Agrarian reforms were one of the first measures proposed in the economic rehabilitation of land.
agronomy n a-gron-o-my: the science and practice of crop production
Many positions in *agronomy* are offered by the Federal Government.
aigrette n ai-grette: feathers worn as a head ornament
Laws had to be passed to prohibit the wearing of *aigrettes* in order to preserve the birds.
ajar adj a-jar: opened slightly
The door to the office was *ajar*.
akimbo adv a-kim-bo: position with hand on hip
He stood *akimbo*, his elbows touching the sides of the hallway.
akimbo adj a-kim-bo: position with hand on hip
He posed in an *akimbo* stance to have his picture taken.
alacrity n a-lac-ri-ty: cheerful briskness
The *alacrity* shown by the new employee gratified the manager.
albino n al-bi-no: white, without pigment
Albinos are extremely rare.
alchemy n al-che-my: medieval chemistry
A goal of *alchemy* was the transmutation of base metals into gold.
alcove n al-cove: small room or nook
The *alcove* was cozy and warm.
alibi n al-i-bi: excuse
The police did not believe his *alibi*.
alibi v al-i-bi: to offer an excuse
She tried to *alibi* herself out of trouble.
alien adj al-ien: foreign
She was an *alien* agent.
alienate v al-ien-ate: to estrange, make inimical or indifferent

One purpose of the offer to the East was to *alienate* the Western nations.

align v a-lign: adjust
They were able to *align* the wheels to stop the shake.

allay v al-lay: to pacify, calm
Therapy will often *allay* the fears of the neurotic.

allegation n al-le-ga-tion: assertion without proof
He was unable to prove his wild *allegations*.

allegory n al-le-go-ry: a story that teaches through symbols
Animal fables are usually *allegories* of human behavior.

allegro adj al-le-gro: fast, quick (in music)
The conductor asked that they play the *allegro* movement.

alleviate v al-le-vi-ate: to lessen, make easier
The morphine helped to *alleviate* the pain.

alliance n al-li-ance: a union
They created an *alliance* of automobile workers.

allocate v al-lo-cate: to distribute or assign
The new serum was *allocated* among the states by population.

allotment n al-lot-ment: distribution
They quickly used up their *allotment* of sugar.

alloy n al-loy: a mixture of metals
The truck was made from a new *alloy*.

allude v al-lude: to mention indirectly
He *alluded* to their previous conversation.

alluring adj al-lur-ing: attractive, tempting
She was *alluring* in her new dress.

alluvial adj al-lu-vi-al: left by departing water
Alluvial deposits are marked by stratified rock.

aloof adv a-loof: at a distance but in view
At the party, she remained *aloof* and stayed in the corner.

aloof adj a-loof: withdrawn, above
The others considered her too *aloof* to be their friend.

alter v al-ter: to change
The new hair color *altered* her appearance.

altercation n al-ter-ca-tion: a quarrel
After the *altercation* the crowd went home.

alternative adj al-ter-na-tive: choice
The *alternative* means of transportation was to take the train.

altruistic adj al-tru-is-tic: unselfish
He displayed his *altruistic* nature by giving away all of his dinner.

amalgamate v a-mal-gam-ate: to combine
The scientist was able to *amalgamate* the chemicals into a new substance.

amass v a-mass: to accumulate
The snow *amassed* on the ground after the storm.

amatory adj am-a-to-ry: pertaining to sexual love
The *amatory* emphasis in films disturbed some groups.

ambergris n am-ber-gris: intestinal secretion of the sperm whale
A great prize of the whaling expedition was a quantity of *ambergris*.

ambidextrous adj am-bi-dex-trous: able to use both hands equally well
Ambidextrous tennis players have a great advantage.

ambiguous adj am-big-u-ous: unclear
They did not understand her *ambiguous* instructions.

ambulatory adj am-bu-la-to-ry: moving about, able to walk
Ambulatory patients require organized activities to speed their recovery.

ambush n am-bush: a trap
The soldiers were caught in a well-planned *ambush*.

ambush v am-bush: to attack from hiding
The Indians were able to *ambush* their enemies.

ameliorate v a-me-lio-rate: to improve
He was able to *ameliorate* the patient's pain.

amenable adj a-me-na-ble: open to suggestion
He was *amenable* to any proposition.

amend v a-mend: to change, to improve
Make sure to *amend* the contract with the new changes.

amenity n a-men-i-ty: pleasantness, courteous act
One must observe the *amenities* in dealing with strangers.

amicable adj am-i-ca-ble: friendly
The new neighbors were extremely *amicable*.

amnesty n am-nes-ty: pardon
The President granted *amnesty* to the rest of the men.

amorous adj am-o-rous: loving
She was extremely *amorous* to her husband.

ample adj am-ple: large, roomy
He had an *ample* suitcase to carry all of his belongings.

amplify v am-pli-fy: to increase
The guitarist *amplified* his music electronically.

amputate v am-pu-tate: to cut off
The leg had to be *amputated* due to the infection.

amulet n am-u-let: magic charm
She wore the mustard seed *amulet* around her neck.

ancient adj an-cient: old
She purchased the *ancient* table at a good price.

anecdote n an-ec-dote: interesting story
He kept them amused with witty *anecdotes* all evening.

anguish n an-guish: great pain
The *anguish* he suffered from the death of his friend stayed with him for many years.

animate v an-i-mate: to give life to
He was able to *animate* the characters on film.

animate adj an-i-mate: living, active
He grew extremely *animated* when he spoke.

animosity n an-i-mos-i-ty: anger, extreme hatred
He showed his *animosity* by cancelling her contract.

annex v an-nex: to join or add
The Argentines tried to *annex* the Falkland Islands.

annex n an-nex: something added
They built a new *annex* to the hospital.

annihilate v an-ni-hi-late: to destroy
They were all *annihilated* in the savage attack.

annual adj an-nual: yearly
It was an *annual* picnic for the employees.

annul v an-nul: to cancel, make void
The marriage was *annulled* after only a few months.

anode n an-ode: a positive electrode
The wire was connected to the battery's *anode*.

anon adv a-non: soon, shortly
He will be arriving *anon*.

anonymous adj a-non-y-mous: without a name
The book was written by an *anonymous* author.

antagonist n an-tag-o-nist: opponent
The two *antagonists* met in the middle of the ring.

anthracite n an-thra-cite: hard coal
Anthracite is mined in many parts of the world.

antidote n an-ti-dote: a remedy
They immediately gave the child the *antidote* for the poison.

apathetic adj ap-a-thet-ic: indifferent, uncaring
She was *apathetic* about going to the show.

aperture n ap-er-ture: opening
The wider the *aperture* on a camera, the more light can enter.

apex n a-pex: highest point
The man was at the *apex* of his career.

aplomb n a-plomb: poise, assurance
Although he was young, he faced the audience with *aplomb*.

apogee n ap-o-gee: the highest point
The space capsule began to descend after reaching its *apogee*.

apothecary n a-poth-e-car-y: druggist
He purchased pills from the town *apothecary*.

appalling adj ap-pall-ing: horrifying
The child's behavior was *appalling* to her mother.

apparatus n ap-pa-ra-tus: equipment
The magician unloaded his *apparatus* backstage.

apparel n ap-par-el: clothing
They gave their old *apparel* to the charity.

apparition n ap-pa-ri-tion: ghost, phantom
The children were frightened by the *apparition* that appeared in the
room.

appease v ap-pease: to satisfy, allay
The child *appeased* his aunt by being attentive.

append v ap-pend: to attach
He *appended* the paragraph to the end of the story.

appraise v ap-praise: to estimate
He was unable to *appraise* the value of the ring.

apprehend v ap-pre-hend: to capture
The robber was *apprehended* trying to escape.

appropriate adj ap-pro-pri-ate: suitable
She wore an *appropriate* dress for the party.

appropriate v ap-pro-pri-ate: to seize, steal
He *appropriated* the candlestick from the museum.

aptitude n ap-ti-tude: ability, talent
The *aptitude* that he showed on the test was remarkable.

aqueous adj a-que-ous: watery
The ship sunk to its *aqueous* grave.

archaic adj ar-cha-ic: old fashioned
It was an *archaic* style of dance.

arduous adj ar-du-ous: difficult
It was an *arduous* climb up the mountain.

arid adj ar-id: dry, barren
The *arid* desert showed little animal life.

armada n ar-mada: fleet of ships or planes
The American *armada* approached the enemy's coastline.

armistice n ar-mi-stice: a truce
Both sides signed the *armistice* aboard the battleship.

arouse v a-rouse: to awaken, stir up
He was *aroused* by the sound of the marching band.

arrogant adj ar-ro-gant: haughty, proud
The man's *arrogant* behavior embarrassed his wife.

artificial adj ar-ti-fi-cial: not natural
The food contained *artificial* coloring.

ascend v as-cend: to rise, climb
The old man *ascends* the stairs slowly.

asphalt n as-phalt: tar-like substance
His shoes stuck to the hot *asphalt*.

assault n as-sault: an attack
The *assault* upon the fortress was unsuccessful.

assault v as-sault: to attack
He was *assaulted* in front of his own house.

assert v as-sert: declare, defend
He *asserted* himself in the new job and eventually was in complete command.

assiduous adj as-sid-u-ous: persistent
He was *assiduous* in his attempt to learn chemistry.

assimilate v as-sim-i-late: to absorb, digest
The newcomers were quickly *assimilated* into the neighborhood.

assume v as-sume: to take for granted
The man *assumed* that his friend would come back.

assure v as-sure: to make sure of
He tried to *assure* himself that she was on the way.

astonish v as-ton-ish: to surprise, amaze
He was *astonished* at her ability at the piano.

astute adj as-tute: shrewd
She was an *astute* judge of human nature.

atone v a-tone: to make up for
In church, he *atoned* for all his sins.

atrocious adj a-tro-cious: cruel, horrible
He committed an *atrocious* act against the enemy.

attain v at-tain: to reach
He was able to *attain* the fifth level of karate.

attest v at-test: to certify, verify
I *attest* that she was present during the accident.

attire v at-tire: to dress
She liked to *attire* herself in jewelry.

attorney n at-tor-ney: lawyer
They hired a young *attorney* to handle their case.

auction n auc-tion: a public sale
He bought the photograph at the recent *auction*.

auction v auc-tion: to sell publicly
I was able to *auction* off the old car.

audit v au-dit: to examine and check
The CPA *audited* his bank statements to find the error.

audit n au-dit: an examination of financial records
The IRS requested an *audit* for the previous year.

auspicious adj aus-pi-cious: favorable
It was an *auspicious* day to begin his new job.
austere adj aus-tere: harsh, stern
The winter in Canada is extremely *austere*.
authentic adj au-then-tic: reliable, genuine
The painting was *authentic* and signed by the artist.
auxiliary adj aux-il-ia-ry: helping
They joined the *auxiliary* police squadron.
auxiliary n aux-il-ia-ry: an adjunct organization
She was a member of the Ladies' *Auxiliary*.
avarice n av-a-rice: greed
She objected to his *avarice* in business.
avert v a-vert: to avoid
He *averted* his eyes away from his mother.
avid adj av-id: eager, greedy
She was an *avid* reader and took out many books from the library.
aware adj a-ware: watchful, realizing
He was *aware* of the other people looking at him.
awe n awe: feeling of wonder, fear, and reverence
He was in *awe* of the President.
awry adj a-wry: twisted
The road was *awry* as it turned up the mountainside.
axiom n ax-i-om: rule, established principle
He lived by the *axiom* "Do unto others…"
azure adj az-ure: sky-blue
Her coat was *azure* in color.

B

babble v bab-ble: murmur
She could hear the children *babble* as she walked in the room.
badger v badg-er: to annoy, tease
The little girl always *badgered* her brother.
badger n badg-er: a burrowing animal
The mascot of the university is a *badger*.
baffle v baf-fle: to confuse
They tried to *baffle* him with too many clues.

baffle n baf-fle: screen to deflect sound, light, gas, etc.
He removed the *baffle* from the furnace to give off more heat.

baleful adj bale-ful: destructive, deadly
The *baleful* glance of a witch was feared.

ballad n bal-lad: song
She sang a sweet *ballad* to her husband.

banal adj ba-nal: ordinary, trite
The poem was a *banal* example of his work.

baneful adj bane-ful: actively evil
The ex-convict exerted a *baneful* influence on the other members of the group.

banish v ban-ish: to exile, send away
He was *banished* from his homeland forever.

banquet n ban-quet: formal dinner
They wore tuxedos to the *banquet*.

banter n ban-ter: genial teasing
The *banter* between them was purely innocent.

banter v ban-ter: to tease, joke
The children were *bantering* with each other in their room.

barbarous adj bar-ba-rous: uncivilized
The tribe's *barbarous* customs changed little over the years.

bard n bard: poet
Shakespeare was known as the *Bard* of Avon.

baroque adj ba-roque: highly ornate
Baroque decorations are characteristic of the last century.

barren adj bar-ren: empty, fruitless
His house sat on a plot of *barren* land.

barter v bar-ter: to trade
She tried to *barter* with the salesman for the ring.

bastion n bas-tion: a fortress, protected place
The restaurant was a *bastion* of Old World charm.

baton n ba-ton: staff, stick
The drum major passed the *baton* to the person who marched by her side.

bawl v bawl: to cry out
The child began to *bawl* when the music began.

bazaar n ba-zaar: an exchange market place in the East
The *bazaar* is the center of political and social as well as business life in many countries.

beckon v beck-on: to call, signal
He *beckoned* his son to join them.

bedlam n bed-lam: uproar, confusion
The *bedlam* of the pots crashing in the kitchen disturbed his sleep.

befuddle v be-fud-dle: confuse
His explanation only *befuddled* her.

begrudge v be-grudge: to envy, to give reluctantly
He didn't *begrudge* his friend the extra money.

beguile v be-guile: to mislead, deceive
Where he found himself weak, he would *beguile* the opposition into applauding his propositions.

behemoth n be-he-moth: large animal
The elephant was a *behemoth*, bigger than any he had ever seen.

belabor v be-la-bor: to work diligently on, to argue to absurd lengths
The attorney *belabored* the point until the jury was bored.

bellicose adj bel-li-cose: warlike
He was extremely *bellicose* in front of the men.

belligerent adj bel-lig-er-ent: warlike
The two dogs began to grow *belligerent* toward each other.

bellow v bel-low: to roar loudly
The newborn *bellowed* as he entered the world.

bellow n bel-low: a bellowing sound
The *bellow* was heard throughout the city.

benediction n ben-e-dic-tion: blessing
They received the *benediction* at the local church.

benevolent adj be-nev-o-lent: kindly
The *benevolent* old gentleman came to all the parties.

benign adj be-nign: favorable, not malignant
The tumor was *benign* and did not require removal.

bequeath v be-queath: to leave to, to give
He wanted to *bequeath* his money to his children.

berate v be-rate: to scold harshly
She continued to *berate* her children for their error.

bereaved v be-reaved: to be deprived of, usually by death
The widow was *bereaved* by the death of her husband.

beret n be-ret: flat cap
He wore the *beret* at an angle.

berserk adj ber-serk: in a frenzy, crazed
The father went *berserk* when he opened the telephone bill.

beseech v be-seech: to beg, plead with
I *beseech* you to come back home.

besiege v be-siege: to attack
They were *besieged* by black flies while they ate.

bestow v be-stow: to give
He *bestowed* dozens of gifts on his visitors.

bevy n bev-y: small group
  She went to the movies with her *bevy* of friends.
bias v bi-as: prejudice
  The man was *biased* and changed his wife's viewpoint.
bicker v bick-er: to quarrel, argue
  They continued to *bicker* in front of the company.
biennial adj bi-en-ni-al: happening every two years
  Many state legislatures convene on a *biennial* basis.
bigot n big-ot: a prejudiced person
  Her neighbors considered her a *bigot*.
bind v bind: to hold, fasten
  They used the rope to *bind* the packages together.
biped n bi-ped: a two-footed animal
  Those paw prints were made by a *biped*.
blanch v blanch: to whiten, bleach
  The sun *blanched* the laundry hanging on the line.
bland adj bland: agreeable, smooth
  He preferred to eat *bland* food.
blatant adj bla-tant: noisy, obvious
  It was a *blatant* attempt to be noticed.
bleach n bleach: a chemical for removing color
  He used a brand-name *bleach* to take out the stains.
bleach v bleach: to whiten, to use bleach
  She was able to *bleach* the shirts to make them brighter.
bleary adj blear-y: dim, blurred
  After many nights without sleep, he was *bleary* eyed.
blemish n blem-ish: stain, spot, flaw
  The *blemish* first appeared on her cheek and then spread to the rest
  of her face.
blemish v blem-ish: to spoil by a flaw
  The painting was *blemished* by the use of poor lighting.
bliss n bliss: great happiness
  The newlyweds seemed full of *bliss*.
blithe adj blithe: gay, cheerful
  She was considered a *blithe* person, ready for anything.
bloat v bloat: to swell up
  His stomach was *bloated* from all the food he ate.
blotch v blotch: to mark with blotches
  Chicken Pox *blotched* the child's skin.
blotch n blotch: a stain
  There was a dark *blotch* on the tablecloth.
bludgeon n bludg-eon: a short club
  She was hit by a *bludgeon* in back of the head.

bludgeon v bludg-eon: to hit, strike heavily
He was *bludgeoned* into unconsciousness.

blunt adj blunt: dull
He tried to cut the meat with a *blunt* knife.

blunt v blunt: to make dull, take the edge off
She was able to *blunt* his anger by speaking calmly.

blurry adj blur-ry: hazy, unclear
His eyes were *blurry* from the smoke.

blurt v blurt: to say suddenly
The child *blurted* out his name in the middle of the conversation.

bluster v blus-ter: to blow stormily
It was constantly *blustering* outside the cabin.

boar n boar: a male pig or wild hog
They shot a wild *boar* in the jungle.

boast v boast: to brag, praise oneself
The neighbor *boasted* that he had the fastest car on the block.

bogus adj bo-gus: counterfeit, sham
He didn't realize that he had received a *bogus* dollar bill.

boisterous adj bois-ter-ous: cheerfully loud
The crowd grew *boisterous* when the acrobat appeared.

bombastic adj bom-bas-tic: pompous, high-sounding
The *bombastic* politician sounds like a fool on television.

bond n bond: uniting force, agreement
The *bond* was strong between the two friends.

bond v bond: to assure payment
The electrician was *bonded* by his company.

boon n boon: blessing, benefit
The new subway is a *boon* to those in this area.

boor n boor: rude, clumsy individual
Her dinner companion was a noisy *boor*.

botch v botch: bungle, spoil
Because they were careless, they *botched* the job.

bough n bough: tree branch
The apples bent the *bough* to the ground.

boundary n bound-a-ry: limit, border
The *boundary* was at the edge of the river.

bountiful adj boun-ti-ful: abundant, generous
The trees were *bountiful* with fruit.

bouquet n bou-quet: a bunch of flowers
She was surprised at the *bouquet* he brought.

bovine adj bo-vine: cowlike
Persons with a sluggish disposition are called *bovine*.

boycott v boy-cott: to refuse to buy
Due to the high price of grapes, the pickers' crops were *boycotted*.
brace n brace: a couple or pair as applied to dogs, ducks
He owned a *brace* of German shepherds.
brash adj brash: hasty, rash
Don't make *brash* decisions before you think it over.
brawny adj brawn-y: strong, muscular
They used *brawny* young men to paddle the boat.
brazen adj bra-zen: without shame
She was *brazen* in her attempt to get the job.
breach n breach: gap, opening
The water flowed through a *breach* in the dam.
brevity n brev-i-ty: shortness
The *brevity* of the overture made the rest of the musical easy to listen to.
brigand n brig-and: robber
She was stopped along the road by a group of *brigands*.
brim n brim: edge, margin
The coffee cup was filled to the *brim*.
brine n brine: salt water
They soaked the fish in *brine*.
brisk adj brisk: quick and lively
The old man walked in a *brisk* manner.
brittle adj brit-tle: easily broken
Her bones grew *brittle* as she grew older.
brittle n brit-tle: a crisp sugar candy
His daughter made him peanut *brittle* for his trip.
brochure n bro-chure: a pamphlet
Brochures on many topics are available free of charge.
brusque adj brusque: abrupt, blunt
They were put off by his *brusque* behavior.
buccaneer n buc-ca-neer: pirate
The *buccaneer* raided all the towns along the coast.
bucolic adj bu-col-ic: pertaining to a farm, rural
The *bucolic* personality is usually thought of as hearty, simple, and lusty.
buff v buff: to polish
He wanted to *buff* the car with a rag.
buff n buff: dull, brownish yellow
The couch was black and the carpeting was *buff*.
buffoon n buf-foon: clown, fool
He was silly, and they thought he was a *buffoon*.

bulge n bulge: swelling outward
The *bulge* in the can caused them to discard it.
bulge v bulge: to swell out
The box began to *bulge* at the seams.
bulky adj bulk-y: large, ungainly
He wore a *bulky* sweater when he skated.
bullion n bul-lion: gold or silver in the form of bars
Nations exchange *bullion* to pay their trade balances.
bulwark n bul-wark: protection, defense
The men hid behind the stone *bulwark* of the fort.
buoyant adj buoy-ant: floatable
He found his clothing to be *buoyant* in the pool.
burden n bur-den: heavy load, cargo
The *burden* was too large for the mule to carry.
burden v bur-den: to load
He *burdened* himself with too many problems.
burly adj bur-ly: strong, solid
The lumberjack was old, but *burly*.
burnish v bur-nish: to polish by rubbing
Metal that is *burnished* will gleam in the light.
bustle n bus-tle: excitement, activity
He liked the *bustle* in the stores during Christmas.
butt n butt: the object of a jest
The dullard is the *butt* of his classmates' tricks.
buttress v but-tress: strengthen
The wooden supports *buttress* the building.
buttress n but-tress: a structure built against a wall to support
The *buttress* of the church was made of stone.
buxom adj bux-om: plump, jolly
The *buxom* maid is a stock character in many plays.

C

cache n cache: hiding place
The *cache* was later found by the police.
cache v cache: to store or hide
The money was *cached* behind the rock.

cacophony n ca-coph-o-ny:　harsh sounds
He was awakened by the *cacophony* of the chickens.

cadaver n ca-dav-er:　corpse, dead body
They moved the *cadaver* into the other room.

cadence n ca-dence:　rhythm
The drummer set the *cadence* for the rest of the band.

cajole v ca-jole:　to persuade, coax
I tried to *cajole* him into going to the circus.

calamity n ca-lam-i-ty:　great misfortune, disaster
The great flood was a *calamity* that caused suffering to everyone.

caliber n cal-i-ber:　capacity of mind, quality
Men of the highest *caliber* are wanted for these positions.

calk v calk:　to fill a seam with paste
He *calked* the windows to keep the waters from seeping through.

calligraphy n cal-lig-ra-phy:　penmanship
The *calligraphy* of the monks is the basis of many printing typefaces today.

callow adj cal-low:　young, without experience
He was a *callow* lad, just up from the country.

calumniate v ca-lum-ni-ate:　to slander
He was known to *calumniate* anyone who disagreed with him.

camisole n cam-i-sole:　ornamental woman's underbodice
Camisoles return to style periodically when thin blouses are in fashion.

camouflage n cam-ou-flage:　disguise
The man wore his *camouflage* well, and no one recognized him.

camouflage v cam-ou-flage:　to conceal by changing appearance
The wolf was *camouflaged* as a sheep.

candid adj can-did:　frank, sincere
The young girl was *candid* about her feelings.

candor n can-dor:　honesty
He spoke to them with complete *candor*.

canine n ca-nine:　dog
The *canine* bared his teeth as he growled.

canine adj ca-nine:　like a dog
The dentist removed his *canine* teeth.

canister n can-is-ter:　small container
He hid his watch in a wooden *canister*.

canopy n can-o-py:　a cover, shelter
The *canopy* protected them from the rain.

cantankerous adj can-tan-ker-ous:　bad natured
He was a *cantankerous* old man who annoyed everyone.

capacious adj ca-pa-cious: roomy
The *capacious* lobby welcomed us as we entered the hotel.

capitulate v ca-pit-u-late: to surrender
The White Team finally decided to *capitulate* to the Red Team.

capricious adj ca-pri-cious: changeable
She was *capricious* in her moods, and loved to upset everyone.

capsize v cap-size: turn over
The boat *capsized* in the heavy waves.

caption n cap-tion: heading, title
The *caption* under the cartoon was very funny.

captivate v cap-ti-vate: fascinate
The princess *captivated* the heart of the prince.

carafe n ca-rafe: bottle
The *carafe* is now popular for an individual service of coffee.

carbine n car-bine: short rifle
Most of the men in the Old West carried *carbines*.

carcass n car-cass: corpse
They buried the deer's *carcass* beneath the tree.

careen v ca-reen: to tilt, tip
The car began to *careen* off the road.

caress v ca-ress: to embrace, to hug
She *caressed* her daughter's back to calm her.

caress n ca-ress: an affectionate touch, kiss
His *caress* was enough to stop her tears.

caricature n car-i-ca-ture: a distorted sketch
Caricature is the weapon of the political cartoonist.

caries n car-ies: tooth decay
The dentist told her she had a severe case of *caries*.

carmine n car-mine: red or purplish-red color
They painted the room *carmine* and blue.

carnage n car-nage: destruction of life
The *carnage* of modern warfare is frightful to consider.

carom v car-om: bounce off
The car was out of control and *caromed* off the wall.

carom n car-om: a billiard shot
He tried to play a *carom* off the rail.

cartographer n car-tog-ra-pher: map maker
The ancient *cartographers* did not have scientific measuring devices.

casing n cas-ing: covering
It was interesting to watch them pack the sausage into the *casings*.

cask n cask: barrel
The *cask* of wine was taken out of the cellar.

castigate v cas-ti-gate: to criticize severely, to punish

The judge *castigated* the plaintiff before he fined him for contempt of court.

catalyst n cat-a-lyst: substance causing change in other substances

After the scientist added a *catalyst* to the test tube, the rock dissolved.

catastrophe n ca-tas-tro-phe: a calamity, disaster

The recent fire was a *catastrophe* to his family.

catechism n cat-e-chism: elementary book of religious principles

She read from her *catechism* every morning before work.

categorical adj cat-e-gor-i-cal: not conditional, absolute, unqualified

Theirs was a *categorical* surrender.

catholic adj cath-o-lic: universal, widespread

His taste in literature was *catholic*, encompassing all fields.

caucus n cau-cus: meeting

He attended the late-night *caucus*.

caucus v cau-cus: to hold a meeting

They tried to *caucus* during the nomination speeches.

caustic adj caus-tic: biting, stinging

He had a *caustic* sense of humor.

cauterize v cau-ter-ize: to burn to prevent infection

The surgeon *cauterized* the wound, removing dead tissue.

cavalcade n cav-al-cade: procession on horseback

The Queen's *cavalcade* entered the castle before she arrived.

caveat n ca-ve-at: a legal notice preventing some action

A *caveat* may be entered to stop the reading of a will.

cavern n cav-ern: large cave

They hid in the dark *cavern* for two days.

cavity n cav-i-ty: hole, hollow place

He had a *cavity* in his front tooth.

cease v cease: to stop

Please *cease* banging on the table.

cede v cede: surrender, give up

The army *ceded* to the men in the tanks.

celestial adj ce-les-tial: heavenly

The sounds of the harp were almost *celestial*.

celibate adj cel-i-bate: unmarried

He was still *celibate* after all these years.

celibate n cel-i-bate: an unmarried person

The monk remained a *celibate* throughout his life.

censure v cen-sure: to blame, condemn as wrong

The judge *censured* the man for his crime.

censure n cen-sure: formal criticism
He was greatly upset by the *censure*.

chagrin n cha-grin: disappointment
Much to his *chagrin*, nobody showed up at the party.

chalice n chal-ice: cup, goblet
The *chalice* was made of gold and studded with gems.

chaos n cha-os: confusion
The huge hall was filled with *chaos* from all of the soldiers who had entered.

chaperone n chap-er-one: protector, escort, guide
The *chaperone* accompanied the young lovers.

chaperone v chap-er-one: to escort
The man in the tuxedo *chaperoned* the starlet.

char v char: to burn, scorch
The flames *charred* the curtains.

charger n charg-er: horse
She rode proudly upon her white *charger*.

charlatan n char-la-tan: a phony, quack
The doctor was accused of being a *charlatan*.

chasm n chasm: deep hole
The supplies slid down the hill into the dark *chasm*.

chassis n chas-sis: frame or body
The *chassis* of the car was painted red.

chastise v chas-tise: punish, beat
He *chastised* his son for coming home late.

chastity n chas-ti-ty: purity
Everyone in the neighborhood knew of her devotion to *chastity*.

chatter v chat-ter: to talk continually
The two women always *chatter* on the telephone like birds.

cherish v cher-ish: hold dear
She *cherished* her photographs more than her money.

chieftain n chief-tain: leader
He was elected *chieftain* of the tribe.

chimes n chimes: bells
They could hear the *chimes* ringing all day.

chivalrous adj chiv-al-rous: courteous, marked by honesty
His *chivalrous* manner warmed the hearts of all who knew him.

chronic adj chron-ic: continual, constant
She had a *chronic* cough that wasn't helped by her smoking.

churlish adj churl-ish: rude, surly
He was both *churlish* and abrupt in the way in which he chose to deal with the problem.

churn v churn: stir, shake, turn around
The engine continued to *churn* after it was shut off.

churn n churn: container to make butter or cream
She removed the fresh butter from the *churn*.

cicatrix n cic-a-trix: a scar
The doctor found the *cicatrix* behind the patient's ear.

cipher n ci-pher: a code
They were able to understand the *cipher* by using a computer.

circumlocution n cir-cum-lo-cu-tion: talking around a subject
The audience was restive as the speaker's *circumlocution* went on and on.

circumspect adj cir-cum-spect: careful, cautious
The driver was *circumspect* as he turned his car around.

citadel n cit-a-del: fortress, safe place
The horses and men lived in the *citadel* at night.

cite v cite: to quote, to give an example, to refer to or name
She was able to *cite* exactly how the speech was written in the paper.

civil adj civ-il: polite, courteous
She tried to be *civil* to her teacher.

clairvoyance n clair-voy-ance: ESP, insight
The woman was respected for her *clairvoyance*.

clamor n clam-or: loud noise
There was such a *clamor* in the street, they couldn't sleep.

clamor v clam-or: to make a loud noise
They *clamored* for their breakfast.

clandestine adj clan-des-tine: concealed, secret
That was their *clandestine* meeting place.

clatter n clat-ter: confused sounds, noise
The *clatter* came from the back room where the children were playing.

clatter v clat-ter: to make noise
They *clattered* the dishes until we had to leave.

cleave v cleave: to divide, split
He tried to *cleave* the diamond in two halves.

clemency n clem-en-cy: mercy
President Nixon was shown *clemency* by President Ford.

clique n clique: group
He hung around with the *clique* from the East Side.

clutter n clut-ter: a mess, confusion
His apartment was a *clutter* of clothes, dishes, and magazines.

clutter v clut-ter: to put into disorder
She began to *clutter* her bag with her makeup.

coagulate v co-ag-u-late: to thicken
Once the blood *coagulates*, bleeding stops.
coalesce v co-a-lesce: to grow together
The vines *coalesced* as they climbed up the tree.
coax v coax: persuade
Can I *coax* you to buy this suit?
coddle v cod-dle: to pamper
She always *coddled* her dog too much.
coerce v co-erce: to force, compel
She tried to *coerce* them into joining the committee.
cogent adj co-gent: convincing
The lawyer's *cogent* argument easily persuaded the jurors.
cognizant adj cog-ni-zant: aware of
I am fully *cognizant* of your actions yesterday.
cohere v co-here: to connect, stick to
The story just did not *cohere* with the facts.
coherent adj co-her-ent: logically connected
His argument was *coherent* and easy to follow.
cohort n co-hort: a group of people
In the evening, he went to the movies with his *cohorts*.
collision n col-li-sion: crash, conflict
The *collision* of the two trailers blocked the road.
colloquial adj col-lo-qui-al: informal, familiar
It was a *colloquial* saying she had heard before.
comatose adj com-a-tose: unconscious
The patient was *comatose* when they brought him in.
combustible adj com-bus-ti-ble: easily burned
Oil soaked rags are very *combustible*.
comely adj come-ly: attractive
She was a *comely*, young housewife.
commemorate v com-mem-or-ate: to honor
This parade was to *commemorate* Christopher Columbus.
commence v com-mence: to begin
The party will *commence* after dinner.
commerce n com-merce: business, trade
The main *commerce* of the town was exporting sardines.
commiserate v com-mis-er-ate: to console, pity
They came over to *commiserate* with them after the accident.
commotion n com-mo-tion: confusion
The news about the King created a *commotion* in the city.
commute v com-mute: exchange, substitute; to travel
His sentence was *commuted* from life to a full pardon.
He liked *commuting* from the farm to the city.

compact adj com-pact: closely, firmly packed
He drove an American *compact* car.

compact n com-pact: small case containing mirror, powder, etc.
She continually took out her *compact* to put on her makeup.

compact v com-pact: to pack together tightly
He tried to *compact* everything into one box.

compatible adj com-pat-i-ble: agreeable
They reached a *compatible* solution for their difficulties.

compel v com-pel: to force
She tried to *compel* him to attend the party.

competent adj com-pe-tent: qualified
They felt she was *competent* in her typing and gave her the job.

complacent adj com-pla-cent: self-satisfied
He was a *complacent* person, unconcerned about the future.

compliant adj com-pli-ant: yielding
He was completely *compliant* with the doctor.

complicity n com-plic-i-ty: partnership in crime
They were accused of *complicity* in the bank robbery.

comply v com-ply: to accede, yield
I *comply* with your wishes and will stay home.

comportment n com-port-ment: behavior
The teacher criticized the *comportment* of her class.

composure n com-po-sure: calmness
She tried to regain her *composure* after the incident.

compress v com-press: to squeeze together
He was able to *compress* all of the papers into the folder.

compress n com-press: folded cloth or gauze pad
She applied a cold *compress* to his injured eye.

compromise n com-pro-mise: settlement
The *compromise* made between the tenant and the landlord was decided upon in the afternoon.

compromise v com-pro-mise: to settle by negotiation
I will not *compromise* my position.

compulsory adj com-pul-so-ry: required
Mathematics is a *compulsory* subject in High School.

concave adj con-cave: curved inward
The dish was *concave* enough to be able to hold water.

concede v con-cede: to yield, to admit
The candidate *conceded* his defeat to his opponent.

conceit n con-ceit: vanity
The *conceit* she showed made her friends turn away.

conch n conch: large sea shell
You can hear the ocean if you hold the *conch* to your ear.

concise adj con-cise: brief
The report was clear and *concise*.

concoct v con-coct: to prepare
He *concocted* a strange punch from all of the juices.

concord n con-cord: an agreement
The union was able to reach a *concord* with management.

concrete adj con-crete: specific, tangible, real
It was a *concrete*, well-thought-out idea.

concrete n con-crete: solid substance
The stairs were made from poured *concrete*.

condolence n con-do-lence: sympathy
She received their *condolences* when her father died.

condone v con-done: to forgive
I am not able to *condone* what you did the other night.

conducive adj con-du-cive: favorable
It was a *conducive* time to introduce the new product.

conduit n con-duit: passageway, tube
The *conduit* was filled with metal wiring.

confer v con-fer: to consult together
The partners wanted to *confer* before making a decision.

confine v con-fine: to imprison, restrain
He was *confined* to his room for two days.

confirm v con-firm: to prove to be true, verify
The airline called to *confirm* our flight.

confiscate v con-fis-cate: to seize
The illegal cigarettes were *confiscated* by the police.

conflagration n con-fla-gra-tion: large fire
The *conflagration* threatened to spread to the other buildings.

congenial adj con-gen-ial: pleasant, agreeable
He was a *congenial* host, and everyone liked him.

congest v con-gest: to overcrowd
The traffic *congested* the intersection.

conglomeration n con-glom-er-a-tion: a mixture
The meal was a *conglomeration* of various leftovers.

congregate v con-gre-gate: to assemble, gather together
The crowd began to *congregate* around the statue.

conjecture n con-jec-ture: guess, opinion
It was not a fact, only *conjecture*.

conjecture v con-jec-ture: to guess
If you wish to *conjecture*, go right ahead.

connive v con-nive: to cooperate secretly, conspire
They *connived* to cheat the firm of the extra money.

connoisseur n con-nois-seur: expert
He was a *connoisseur* of fine wines.

conscious adj con-scious: knowing, aware
He was *conscious* of the woman next to him.

consecrated v con-se-crat-ed: made sacred
The field behind the church was *consecrated* by the bishop.

consensus n con-sen-sus: general agreement
It is the *consensus* of this club to raise the dues.

consequence n con-se-quence: a result
He is responsible for the *consequences* of his bad manners.

conserve v con-serve: to preserve, protect
It is important to *conserve* water during the shortage.

console v con-sole: to comfort
Each time she would cry, the puppy would *console* her.

console n con-sole: a cabinet, desk, or storage space
The *console* was made of walnut.

conspire v con-spire: to plot
The men *conspired* to overthrow the government.

constitute v con-sti-tute: to make up, to form
These three pieces *constitute* the entire collection.

constrict v con-strict: to compress, squeeze
She felt *constricted* by the small belt.

construe v con-strue: explain, interpret
From the evidence, he was able to *construe* what actually happened.

consume v con-sume: use up, eat
The two of them *consumed* all of the cake.

contemplate v con-tem-plate: to think about
He *contemplated* all day long and then made his move.

contend v con-tend: to fight, struggle for; to claim
They were going to *contend* for the world championship.
I *contend* that I am right.

contention n con-ten-tion: belief, claim
It was her *contention* that the painting was worth more.

contingent adj con-tin-gent: dependent on, associated with
His arrival is *contingent* upon getting through Customs quickly.

contingent n con-tin-gent: a group of people, troops
The entire *contingent* moved its operations down river.

contort v con-tort: to twist
His face was *contorted* with pain.

contrary adj con-trary: opposite
His opinion was *contrary* to what his friends believed.

contrive v con-trive: invent
His excuse seemed totally *contrived*.

controversy n con-tro-ver-sy: a quarrel, disagreement
He could not resolve the *controversy* between them.
convalesce v con-va-lesce: to recover strength
He was able to *convalesce* at home after his illness.
convene v con-vene: to meet, assemble
The group *convened* in the school yard.
convert v con-vert: to change
He was able to *convert* the dollars into pesos.
convert n con-vert: a person who has changed beliefs, religions
She was a *convert* to Christianity.
convey v con-vey: to carry
I will *convey* your message to your mother.
convivial adj con-viv-i-al: sociable
It was a small group of *convivial* people.
convoy n con-voy: small group
There was a *convoy* of ships in the North Atlantic Ocean.
convoy v con-voy: to escort
The man was able to *convoy* the trucks cross-country.
convulse v con-vulse: to shake
The child began to *convulse* from the fever.
cope v cope: to struggle and succeed
She *coped* well after the death of her husband.
copious adj co-pi-ous: plentiful, abundant
She took *copious* notes during the lecture.
coquette n co-quette: a flirt
She was a well-known *coquette* in Paris.
cordial adj cor-dial: friendly, sincere
The children appeared *cordial* to the visitors.
cordial n cor-dial: alcoholic drink
After dinner, he served *cordials* to his guests.
corpulent adj cor-pu-lent: fat
His *corpulent* body was sprawled across the chair.
corridor n cor-ri-dor: hallway
There was a *corridor* between the children's rooms.
corrupt adj cor-rupt: evil, wicked
He was the most *corrupt* ruler they ever knew.
cosmos n cos-mos: the universe
The stars twinkled throughout the *cosmos*.
council n coun-cil: group of people
He was a member of the local safety *council*.
counsel n coun-sel: advice, lawyer
The *counsel* met with the prisoner in his cell.

counsel v coun-sel: to give advice
I will *counsel* him with his problem.

course n course: direction, school subject
He followed the *course* of the road to the next town.

covenant n cov-e-nant: a contract, agreement
They signed a *covenant* before their wedding.

covert adj cov-ert: secret
It was a *covert* operation, designed to suprise the enemy.

covet v co-vet: to desire enviously
He *coveted* all the items and would not share with his sister.

cower v cow-er: hide, crouch in fear
The cat *cowered* in the corner when the dog walked by.

cowl n cowl: hood
He pulled a *cowl* around his head for warmth.

coy adj coy: shy
The child acted *coy* in front of the strangers.

crass adj crass: gross, stupid
It was a *crass* remark to make to your father.

crave v crave: to desire, yearn for
He *craved* a piece of chocolate cake.

craven adj cra-ven: cowardly
His actions labeled him a *craven* individual.

credible adj cred-i-ble: believable
His story was not entirely *credible*.

cremate v cre-mate: to burn to ashes
The body was *cremated* and the ashes scattered over the ocean.

crestfallen adj crest-fall-en: upset, discouraged
They were *crestfallen* they did not get the house they wanted.

crevice n cre-vice: crack
The *crevice* was where the spiders lived.

crimson adj crim-son: dark red
Her face turned *crimson* with embarrassment.

cringe v cringe: to crouch in fear
The dog *cringed* in the corner.

criterion n cri-te-ri-on: rule, a standard
His *criterion* for success was much higher than hers.

crochet v cro-chet: to knit
She *crocheted* the yellow yarn into a sweater.

crony n cro-ny: friend, pal
He and his old *crony* played cards all day.

croon v croon: to sing
He *crooned* love songs to her as he paddled the canoe.

crouch v crouch: to stoop, bend
He *crouched* behind the bush to avoid being seen.
crucial adj cru-cial: extremely important
The last play was the most *crucial* of the second half.
crucible n cru-ci-ble: a container
They were able to carry the food in a small *crucible*.
crude adj crude: raw, unrefined
The *crude* sugar was sent to be refined.
crude n crude: unrefined petroleum
The *crude* was taken from deep beneath the ground.
crypt n crypt: tomb, vault
They discovered the gold buried in the ancient *crypt*.
cue n cue: hint, suggestion
Let me give you a *cue* about the new boss.
cue v cue: to give a hint to
The actor *cued* the actress, but forgot his own lines.
culinary adj cu-li-nar-y: pertaining to food, cooking
The table was spread with assorted *culinary* delights.
cull v cull: to select, choose
He tried to *cull* the broken toys from the collection.
culminate v cul-mi-nate: to result
The argument *culminated* in a fist fight.
cult n cult: group, religious system
The *cult* carried the message to all the people.
cumbersome adj cum-ber-some: hard to manage
Its size made the package *cumbersome* for the woman.
cunning adj cun-ning: skillful, clever
He was a *cunning* hunter.
cunning n cun-ning: slyness, craftiness
She was known for her *cunning*.
cur n cur: worthless person or dog
He was a vicious *cur*, and they had to give him away.
curb v curb: to restrain
The owner was asked to *curb* his dog.
curb n curb: stone street edge
The *curb* of the street was cracked and broken.
curriculum n cur-ric-u-lum: a program of studies, courses
The new *curriculum* included several new courses.
curt adj curt: brief and rude, short
She was *curt* with her friend, which surprised both of them.
curtail v cur-tail: to shorten, lessen
The trip was *curtailed* due to the man's illness.

custom n cus-tom: habit, usual action
It was her *custom* to feed the children after school.
custom adj cus-tom: made to order
He enjoyed wearing *custom* shirts from his tailor.
cyclic adj cy-clic: periodic
His appearance at the show was on a *cyclic* basis.
cyclone n cy-clone: windstorm
The *cyclone* tore through the house like it was made of paper.
cynical adj cyn-i-cal: sneering, sarcastic
He was *cynical* about their ability to finish the project.

D

daft adj daft: silly, crazy
The people in town considered him a little *daft*.
dainty n dain-ty: something special
He picked out the *dainty* from the selected candies.
dainty adj dain-ty: delicate
He refused to sit on the *dainty* seat.
dais n da-is: platform
The chairman stood on the *dais* and waved to the crowd.
dale n dale: a small valley
He trudged over hill and *dale*.
damask n dam-ask: a fine fabric with a figured weave
The crystal bowls were displayed on a fine *damask*.
dank adj dank: damp, moist
The cave was dark and *dank*.
dapper adj dap-per: neat, trim
Despite his age, he always looked *dapper*.
dappled adj dap-pled: marked with small spots
The *dappled* horse won the race.
dastard n das-tard: complete coward
He was a *dastard* and a cheat.
data n da-ta: information
He received the latest *data* on the project.
dauntless adj daunt-less: fearless, brave
The men were *dauntless* in their quest for the gold.

davit n dav-it: a crane for hoisting boats
The *davit* supported the lifeboats.

dawdle v daw-dle: to waste time, trifle
Do not *dawdle* at your tasks.

de facto adj de fac-to: actual as opposed to legal
Although the *de facto* government was not duly elected, it was in power.

deacon n dea-con: clergyman
The *deacon* gave a long, tiresome sermon.

dearth n dearth: scarcity
There was a *dearth* of grain last year in Russia.

debacle n de-ba-cle: disaster
The final battle was a *debacle* for the English.

debase v de-base: to degrade
She felt *debased* by the criticism.

debate v de-bate: to discuss
They continued to *debate* the issue long after it was over.

debate n de-bate: a discussion of opposing reasons
The candidates were featured in the *debate* on TV.

debauch v de-bauch: to corrupt
The temptations they offered could not *debauch* her.

debilitate v de-bil-i-tate: to weaken
He was *debilitated* from lack of food.

debonair adj deb-o-nair: courteous
Suave and *debonair*, the gentleman impressed the ladies with his city manners.

debut n de-but: first appearance
Her *debut* as a violinist was well attended.

decade n dec-ade: ten-year period
At the end of her sixth *decade*, they had a large party.

decadence n de-ca-dence: decay
The *decadence* of the neighborhood upset the visitors.

decamp v de-camp: to depart suddenly
The patrol prepared to *decamp* before daylight.

decant v de-cant: pour out, pour off
It is important to *decant* the wine well before you serve it.

decanter n de-cant-er: ornamental wine bottle
They poured port from the *decanter*.

decapitate v de-cap-i-tate: to behead
During the French Revolution, people were *decapitated*.

deciduous adj de-cid-u-ous: leaf-sheddng
Most trees are *deciduous*, but evergreens retain their foliage throughout the winter.

decipher v de-ci-pher: to interpret, decode
He was able to *decipher* the enemy's code book.
declivity n de-cliv-i-ty: downward slope
The *declivity* offered fine skiing.
decolleté adj de-col-le-té: low-necked
The *decolleté* dress attracted much attention from the men.
decompose v de-com-pose: to decay, rot
The tree began to *decompose* shortly after it died.
decorous adj dec-o-rous: proper
Decorous conduct is the mark of a gentleman.
decoy n de-coy: a lure
They used a *decoy* to attract the ducks to the pond.
decoy v de-coy: to trick, fool
He tried to *decoy* his opponent into running to the left.
decrepit adj de-crep-it: old, feeble
They finally sold their *decrepit* car.
decry v de-cry: to blame, condemn
He *decried* his fate upon his illness.
deduce v de-duce: to derive by reasoning
From the facts presented, we *deduce* this conclusion.
deduct v de-duct: to subtract
The bank *deducted* their monthly service charge.
deem v deem: to have an opinion, think
They did not *deem* him worthy of the honors he received.
deface v de-face: to spoil, mar
The students *defaced* the wall of the school.
defame v de-fame: to destroy one's reputation, slander
The politician was *defamed* by the reporter's remarks.
default v de-fault: to fail to pay
Unfortunately, he *defaulted* on his loan.
defect v de-fect: to desert
He planned to *defect* from his country.
defect n de-fect: a flaw
The diamond contained a *defect* and was worthless.
defer v de-fer: to put off
I'd like to *defer* my opinion until I've heard the arguments.
deficit n def-i-cit: shortage
The auditor uncovered a *deficit* in their bank balance.
defile v de-file: to befoul, make profane
A man is not allowed to wear shoes in a mosque, lest he *defile* it.
deflect v de-flect: to turn away
The steel plate *deflected* the bullet.

defraud v de-fraud: to cheat
He tried to *defraud* the bank by changing the records.
deft adj deft: nimble
His fingers were *deft* as he tied the knots.
defunct adj de-funct: extinct
That railroad line has been *defunct* for a long time.
degenerate v de-gen-er-ate: grow worse
Without medical care, you will *degenerate* quickly.
degenerate n de-gen-er-ate: low person, one who has fallen to
a lower state
He was a *degenerate* person and to be avoided.
degrade v de-grade: demote, lower
After the poor performance, his job status was *degraded*.
dehydrated adj de-hy-drat-ed: without water
The man was *dehydrated* after running in the marathon.
deify v de-i-fy: to make as a god
They would *deify* Caesar.
deign v deign: to condescend
He *deigned* to reply to their criticism.
deity n de-i-ty: god, goddess
In ancient Greece they worshipped many *deities*.
delectable adj de-lec-ta-ble: delightful
The food is delicious, the girls *delectable*, and the music delirious.
delegate v del-e-gate: to appoint
He was *delegated* to be the first speaker.
delegate n del-e-gate: representative
The country's *delegate* spoke at the meeting.
delete v de-lete: leave out, omit
If you *delete* that word, the sentence will be clearer.
deleterious adj del-e-te-ri-ous: injurious, harmful
DDT, when taken internally, has a *deleterious* effect on the body.
deliberate adj de-lib-er-ate: unhurried, intentional
It was a *deliberate* act, intended to anger them.
deliberate v de-lib-er-ate: to consider carefully
They *deliberated* for two hours before making their decision.
delineate v de-lin-e-ate: to mark off the boundary of
They asked him to *delineate* the areas where play was permitted.
delude v de-lude: to trick, mislead
She was *deluded* into believing the job was easy.
deluge n del-uge: a flood, overflowing
Noah was the only one to escape the *deluge*.
deluge v del-uge: to flood, to overwhelm
They were *deluged* by the quantity of gifts.

demagogue n dem-a-gogue: false leader
He was only a *demagogue*, and nobody respected him.
demean v de-mean: to humble
I don't want to *demean* you, only caution you.
demeanor n de-mean-or: behavior
His child's calm *demeanor* was appropriate for the wedding.
demented adj de-ment-ed: crazy
He acted as if he were *demented*, and he was locked up.
demise n de-mise: death
His early *demise* was truly surprising.
demote v de-mote: to lower in rank
The soldier was *demoted* for his failure to perform properly.
demur v de-mur: to hesitate, object
Once he *demurred*, we knew we had the advantage of additional time to prepare.
demure adj de-mure: serious, sober
The *demure* maiden was an object of their admiration, but not their affection.
denizen n den-i-zen: occupant
The parrot was a *denizen* of the rain forest.
dense adj dense: thick
The children became lost in the *dense* forest.
depict v de-pict: show, to portray
His role was to *depict* a Frenchman.
deplete v de-plete: to empty, exhaust
We do not want to *deplete* our entire oil supply.
deplore v de-plore: to regret, to grieve for
He *deplored* the soldiers' attack on the village.
deploy v de-ploy: to position, spread out
The outfield was *deployed* for the batter at the plate.
deport v de-port: to exile, send away
He was *deported* to his native country.
depot n de-pot: station, warehouse
The train was standing in the *depot*.
depraved adj de-praved: sordid, corrupt
Only a *depraved* mind would think of committing a heinous crime.
deprecate v dep-re-cate: to detract from
Do not *deprecate* what you cannot understand.
depreciate v de-pre-ci-ate: to lessen in value
Property will *depreciate* rapidly unless kept in good repair.
deranged adj de-ranged: insane, disordered
The working of the *deranged* mind baffles even those trained in mental care.

derelict adj der-e-lict: abandoned
The building was old and *derelict*.

derelict n der-e-lict: worthless person
The *derelict* stood begging on the corner.

deride v de-ride: to make fun of, ridicule
The boys *derided* him because he could not ride a horse.

derivation n der-i-va-tion: origin, root
It is fun to learn the *derivation* of words.

descend v de-scend: to go down; derived from
He *descended* the stairs slowly.
She is *descended* from a long line of jewelers.

descry v des-cry: to pry out, discover by eye
In the distance we could *descry* a small cabin.

designate v des-ig-nate: to indicate
I will *designate* you to take charge of the party.

designate n des-ig-nate: person chosen for a specific task
He is the *designate* for the new office manager.

desist v de-sist: to stop
I wish you would *desist* from constantly calling me.

desolate adj des-o-late: cheerless, empty, barren
The area was *desolate* and lonely.

desolate v des-o-late: to lay waste to
The fire *desolated* the entire block of houses.

despair n de-spair: loss of hope
She was filled with *despair* after her accident.

despair v de-spair: to lose hope
He began to *despair* that he would ever see her again.

despise v de-spise: to dislike intensely
She *despised* him for his ill manners.

despot n des-pot: tyrant
Stalin was one of the worst *despots* in history.

destitute adj des-ti-tute: poor
The family was *destitute* after the flood destroyed their home.

destitution n des-ti-tu-tion: poverty
They lived in complete *destitution*, without any income.

detain v de-tain: to hold back
They were unable to *detain* the train any longer.

deter v de-ter: to hinder, stop one from doing something
If you continue to *deter* me from my goal, I will never finish.

detergent n de-ter-gent: cleanser
She washed the dishes with a less abrasive *detergent*.

deteriorate v de-te-ri-o-rate: to grow worse
The building began to *deteriorate* from lack of upkeep.

determine v de-ter-mine: to decide
He was unable to *determine* which job to choose.
detest v de-test: to hate
I *detest* having to eat fish.
detonate v det-o-nate: to cause to explode
The bomb was *detonated* under the house.
detract v de-tract: to take away
His dirty shoes *detracted* from his new tie.
detrimental adj det-ri-men-tal: harmful
Artificial supplements are *detrimental* to your health.
devastate v dev-as-tate: to ruin, destroy
The community was *devastated* by the epidemic.
deviate v de-vi-ate: to turn aside
His new attitude caused him to *deviate* from his goal.

device n de-vice: a plan, a mechanical apparatus
The new *device* was able to turn on the lights by itself.
devise v de-vise: to plan, contrive
She *devised* a plan to escape.
devour v de-vour: to eat hungrily
The children began to *devour* the sandwiches immediately.
dew n dew: moisture
The *dew* on the morning grass soaked their shoes.
dexterous adj dex-ter-ous: skillful, expert
He was extremely *dexterous* at juggling.
diabolic adj di-a-bol-ic: devilish, fiendish
The ancients used charms to ward off the influence of *diabolic*
creatures.
dialogue n di-a-logue: conversation
They continued their *dialogue* on the way to work.
diaphanous adj di-aph-a-nous: almost transparent, sheer
Her *diaphanous* negligee revealed the outlines of a beautiful figure.
diction n dic-tion: style of speech
His *diction* was easily understood.

dictum n dic-tum: an authoritative statement
The professor's *dictum* ended the debate.
didactic adj di-dac-tic: instructive, intended to teach
The *didactic* approach may be well suited for a textbook but should
be avoided in other books.
diffident adj dif-fi-dent: reserved, shy, timid
They grew used to his *diffident* behavior.
diffuse adj dif-fuse: spread, scattered
It was a *diffuse* vapor that covered the city.

diffuse v dif-fuse: to spread in many directions
He tried to *diffuse* the crowd's anger by telling jokes.
dignity n dig-ni-ty: worth, nobleness
He sat with *dignity* upon the throne.
digress v di-gress: to turn aside
I'd like to *digress* a moment in my discussion with you.
dilapidated adj di-lap-i-dat-ed: rundown, decayed
She lived in a *dilapidated* building across town.
dilate v di-late: to swell, enlarge
His pupils *dilated* from the drops the doctor used.
dilemma n di-lem-ma: difficult choices or situation
His *dilemma* was solved by his boss, who made the decision for him.
dilettante n dil-et-tante: aimless follower of the fine arts
A *dilettante* may be more interested in talking of his artistic pursuits
than following them.
diligent adj dil-i-gent: hard working
He was extremely *diligent* at the job.
dilute v di-lute: to weaken
He felt it was better to serve *diluted* drinks.
diminish v di-min-ish: to lessen, reduce
Their supply of food slowly began to *diminish*.
din n din: noise
She couldn't hear over the *din*.
dingy adj din-gy: dirty and dark
He felt uncomfortable in the *dingy* hallway.
dirigible n dir-i-gi-ble: a blimp
The old *dirigibles* were filled with helium.
disarray n dis-ar-ray: disorder, confusion
Her room was in complete *disarray*.
disaster n dis-as-ter: terrible tragedy
The airplane crash was one of the worst *disasters* in history.
disavow v dis-a-vow: to deny
I *disavow* any knowledge of their plot.
disburse v dis-burse: pay, expend
The checks were *disbursed* at noon.
discard v dis-card: to cast aside
He planned to *discard* the old sweater.
discard n dis-card: something thrown aside
Her dress was originally a *discard* from the factory.
discern v dis-cern: to recognize
I am able to *discern* the truth when I hear it.
disciple n dis-ci-ple: pupil, follower
He was a *disciple* of the great philosopher.

disclaim v dis-claim: to renounce, give up claim to
In order to obtain United States citizenship, one must *disclaim* any title from another nation.

discord n dis-cord: disagreement
The only *discord* between them was the meeting place.

discourse v dis-course: to talk
He was able to *discourse* on any subject.

discourse n dis-course: a speech
After hearing her *discourse* for an hour, I left.

discreet adj dis-creet: cautious, secretive
The couple was *discreet* about their relationship.

discrete adj dis-crete: separate, distinct
These were two *discrete* events, totally unrelated.

discretion n dis-cre-tion: power of decision, individual judgment
The penalty to be imposed is often left to the *discretion* of the judge.

disdain v dis-dain: to regard as beneath one's dignity
He *disdained* the actions of his peers.

disinfect v dis-in-fect: to kill germs
The nurse sprayed the room to *disinfect* it.

disingenuous adj dis-in-gen-u-ous: sophisticated, not innocent
The slip of the tongue indicated that he was not as *disingenuous* as he wished to appear.

disinterested adj dis-in-ter-est-ed: not involved in, unprejudiced
A *disinterested* witness is one who has no personal involvement in the outcome of the matter.

disjointed adj dis-joint-ed: disconnected, dislocated
The story was so *disjointed*, it was unbelievable.

dismal adj dis-mal: gloomy
After two weeks of rain, he felt as *dismal* as the weather.

disparage v dis-par-age: to belittle
The father continually *disparaged* his son's ideas.

disparity n dis-par-i-ty: difference
There was a great *disparity* in their ages.

dispatch v dis-patch: send off
They were given their orders and *dispatched* to the coast.

dispatch n dis-patch: a message, speed
They received an urgent *dispatch* from the general.

dispel v dis-pel: to scatter, cast away
I want to *dispel* your fear about air travel.

disperse v dis-perse: to scatter, spread out
Their children were *dispersed* throughout the country.

dispute v dis-pute: to argue or debate
They began to *dispute* ownership of the baseball.
dispute n dis-pute: a debate or quarrel
Neither of them won the *dispute*.
dissect v dis-sect: cut apart
In biology, the students *dissected* a frog.
disseminate v dis-sem-i-nate: to scatter
The literature was *disseminated* to the crowd.
dissension n dis-sen-sion: quarreling
The *dissension* between them was enough to cause their breakup.
dissertation n dis-ser-ta-tion: a formal essay
The *dissertation* is an important requirement for an advanced degree.
dissipate v dis-si-pate: to scatter, spread, dissolve
The seeds were *dissipated* throughout the countryside.

dissolute adj dis-so-lute: immoral
The *dissolute* young man was soon without friends or reputation.
dissonant adj dis-so-nant: harsh sounding
The music was *dissonant* and hard to appreciate.
dissuade v dis-suade: to advise against, divert by persuasion
His friends *dissuaded* him from that unwise plan of action.
distend v dis-tend: to enlarge, expand, stretch
The balloon was *distended* from too much air, and it burst.

distinct adj dis-tinct: clear; separate
There was a *distinct* pattern of footprints in the mud.
The husband and wife had *distinct* lives of their own.
distortion n dis-tor-tion: a twisting out of shape; misstating of facts
The *distortions* by the historians left little of the man's true character for posterity.
Polio caused *distortion* of the limbs.

distraught adj dis-traught: upset, confused
He was *distraught* about losing the game.
diva n di-va: prima donna, a leading woman singer in opera
The *diva* took another bow.
divan n di-van: couch, sofa
They sat beside each other on the old *divan*.

diverge v di-verge: to extend in different directions
The map showed a main lode with thin veins *diverging* in all directions.
diverse adj di-verse: unlike, different
His furniture was a collection of *diverse* periods.

divest v di-vest: to deprive, strip
After the court martial, he was *divested* of his rank and decorations.
divulge v di-vulge: make known
Don't *divulge* any of the information to your brother.
docile adj doc-ile: easily managed
Although he looked wild, the lion was really *docile*.
doff v doff: to remove
He *doffed* his hat to all the women.
dogma n dog-ma: belief, doctrine
The *dogma* that he followed was based on a strict code of ethics.
dogmatic adj dog-mat-ic: opinionated
His *dogmatic* statements were not supported by evidence.
dole n dole: a free distribution of food or money
Some people live on the *dole*.
doleful adj dole-ful: sad, dismal
His *doleful* expression told the entire story of his misfortune.
domain n do-main: territory
The dog's entire *domain* was the backyard.
domestic adj do-mes-tic: tame, of the home
She owned a rare *domestic* cat.
domestic n do-mes-tic: a maid, cook, household worker
She worked as a *domestic* when she was younger.
domicile n dom-i-cile: residence, home
He continued to change his legal *domicile* to avoid creditors.
dominant adj dom-i-nant: controlling
She was the *dominant* one in their relationship.
don v don: to put on
He wanted to *don* the robe before the ceremony.
dormant adj dor-mant: inactive, out of use
The plan was *dormant* for five years until it was revived.
dorsal adj dor-sal: on the back
They could see the shark's *dorsal* fin cut through the water.
dossier n dos-si-er: file on a subject or person
The French police kept a *dossier* on every person with a criminal record.
dotard n do-tard: senile person
The old man is a *dotard*.
doting adj dot-ing: foolishly fond
Rhett Butler was a *doting* father.
dour adj dour: gloomy, sullen
He was a *dour* person and no fun to be with.
douse v douse: to drench, soak
The fireman *doused* the embers to make sure the fire was out.

dowdy adj dow-dy: shabby
She wore a *dowdy*, old dress to the party.
downy adj down-y: fluffy
The quilt was soft and *downy*.
drab adj drab: dull, monotonous
The entire room was decorated in *drab* colors.
drench v drench: to soak
She was *drenched* from the sudden rainstorm.
drivel n driv-el: saliva running from the mouth
She wiped away her daughter's *drivel* and stopped her tears.
drivel v driv-el: to slobber
The baby continued to *drivel* on his shirt.
droll adj droll: quaint, amusingly different
He had a *droll* sense of humor that wasn't always appreciated.
dross n dross: waste matter, scum
The process of separating the valuable metal from the *dross* may be too expensive to do.
drought n drought: dry weather
Many crops died during the *drought* from lack of water.
drowsy adj drow-sy: sleepy
He grew *drowsy* from all the food and drinks.
drudgery n drudg-er-y: unpleasant work
I always found that cleaning the house was *drudgery*.
dubious adj du-bi-ous: doubtful
I am extremely *dubious* about your solution.
duct n duct: tube, pipe
The engineers designed new heating *ducts* for the house.
dupe v dupe: to deceive, fool
She was easily *duped* by his calm manner.
dupe n dupe: a person easily tricked
He was merely a *dupe* in their secret plans.
durable adj dur-able: able to exist, lasting
The table was covered with a *durable* cloth.
dusky adj dusk-y: obscure, dim
It was a *dusky* light in the room, and hard to see.
dwell v dwell: to reside
Bears *dwell* in their dens.
dwindle v dwin-dle: shrink, diminish
As the puddle dried up in the sunlight, it *dwindled* from sight.

E

earnest adj ear-nest: serious, grave
   It was an *earnest* opinion from someone who cared.
ebb v ebb: to decline
   His strength began to *ebb* as he grew older.
ebb adj ebb: shallow, low
   The boats were stuck in the mud during *ebb* tide.
ebullience n e-bul-lience: a boiling up, overflow
   The *ebullience* of youth can be wearying to older persons.
eccentric adj ec-cen-tric: odd, peculiar
   His approach to the problem was *eccentric*, but it worked.
eccentric n ec-cen-tric: a peculiar person
   The wealthy, old *eccentric* lived in a tent.
eclectic adj ec-lec-tic: drawing from diverse sources or systems
   His *eclectic* record collection included everything from Bach cantatas
   to punk rock.
eclogue n ec-logue: pastoral poem
   The poet recited her *eclogue* to the audience.
ecology n e-col-o-gy: science of life's relation to environment
   Persons concerned about *ecology* are worried about the pollution of
   the earth's environment.
ecstasy n ec-sta-sy: great pleasure
   She was in *ecstasy* over her recent promotion.
eddy n ed-dy: whirlpool
   The ship was caught in the *eddy* beneath the bridge.
edible adj ed-i-ble: fit to be eaten
   If the milk has soured, then it is no longer *edible*.
edict n e-dict: a public notice issued by authority
   The *edict* issued by the junta dissolved the government.
edification n ed-i-fi-ca-tion: instruction
   He repeated the material for his son's *edification*.
edifice n ed-i-fice: building
   The stone *edifice* stood taller than the other buildings.
educe v e-duce: to elicit, draw out
   Can you *educe* any information from her notes?
eerie adj ee-rie: mysterious
   The *eerie* quality of the house made us feel that it might be haunted.
efficient adj ef-fi-cient: capable, competent
   She was a very *efficient* office worker.

effigy n ef-fi-gy: image, statue
The team burned an *effigy* of their coach.

effrontery n ef-fron-tery: shameless audacity
He was suprised at the man's *effrontery* to him.

effusive adj ef-fu-sive: gushing, demonstrative
Her *effusive* greeting seemed overdone.

ego n e-go: self
He was so absorbed by his own *ego* that he lost all of his friends.

egress n e-gress: exit
When you leave, use the *egress* at the rear of the building.

elaborate adj e-lab-o-rate: detailed, complicated
The decorations were *elaborate* and festive.

elaborate v e-lab-o-rate: to work out in detail
He *elaborated* on how he planned to design the house.

elastic adj e-las-tic: stretchable
The *elastic* waistband on the pants made them comfortable to wear.

elastic n e-las-tic: an elastic band or fabric
The *elastic* in her hair held her ponytail together.

elate v e-late: to make happy, joyful
He was *elated* at the news of his promotion.

elicit v e-lic-it: draw forth
I was not able to *elicit* a response from him.

elongate v e-lon-gate: to stretch
They *elongated* the cord as far as it could go.

eloquence n el-o-quence: graceful speech
His *eloquence* was enjoyed by all who listened.

elucidate v e-lu-ci-date: to explain, clarify
Perhaps if you *elucidate* more, I will understand.

elude v e-lude: avoid, evade
The man was able to *elude* the posse.

emaciated adj e-ma-ci-at-ed: thin, lean
He was tall and *emaciated* looking.

emanate v em-a-nate: to derive from, issue forth
American law *eminates* largely from English common law.

emancipate v e-man-ci-pate: set free
By opening the cage door, the zookeeper *emancipated* the lions inside.

embargo n em-bar-go: restriction
The U.S. imposed a grain *embargo*, and couldn't ship anything.

embellish v em-bel-lish: adorn, decorate
The tassels *embellished* the hat.

embezzle v em-bez-zle: to steal
The man *embezzled* the money from the cash register.

embolism n em-bo-lism: blood clot
Embolisms, now known to be responsible for many heart attacks, are preventable with certain drugs.

emboss v em-boss: to decorate, engrave
His case was *embossed* with his initials.

emetic n e-met-ic: an agent inducing vomiting
An *emetic* is prescribed for most poisons taken by mouth.

eminent adj em-i-nent: distinguished, evident
The *eminent* speaker approached the podium.

emissary n em-is-sar-y: agent, representative
He was an *emissary* from another country.

emit v e-mit: give off, send out
The sound that the horn *emits* can be heard several miles away.

emollient adj e-mol-lient: soothing
An *emollient* lotion is good for sunburn.

emolument n e-mol-u-ment: reward for work
Teachers receive comparatively greater *emoluments* in the Soviet Union than in the United States.

emphatic adj em-phat-ic: forceful
Mother was *emphatic* when she told us not to eat the cake.

emporium n em-po-ri-um: marketplace
The *emporium* was filled with fresh fruit and vegetables.

emulate v em-u-late: to vie with, try to equal
He tried to *emulate* the feats of the older boys.

encounter v en-coun-ter: to meet
While driving his jeep, he *encountered* a train.

encroach v en-croach: trespass
The man *encroached* upon the stranger's territory.

endeavor v en-deav-or: to attempt, strive
He *endeavored* to win the race and was successful.

endeavor n en-dcav-or: an attempt to accomplish something
It was a very difficult *endeavor*, but he volunteered anyway.

endemic adj en-dem-ic: peculiar to or prevalent in an area or group
Malaria is *endemic* in many southern countries.

endure v en-dure: tolerate, last
How long could he continue to *endure* the pain?

enervate v e-ner-vate: weaken
She was *enervated* by the hot sunshine.

engender v en-gen-der: produce, cause
Don't *engender* trouble by starting an argument.

engross v en-gross: occupy fully

The book *engrossed* her so much that she didn't have time to do any of her chores.

engulf v en-gulf: to swallow up
The rising waters *engulfed* the villiage.

enhance v en-hance: to add to, to make greater
Additional make-up *enhanced* her beauty.

enigma n e-nig-ma: puzzle
Her face was an *enigma* and confused her friends.

enjoin v en-join: to urge
I *enjoin* you to complete the application.

enmity n en-mity: hatred
They shared an *enmity* for the director.

ennui n en-nui: boredom
He was exhausted from the *ennui* he felt.

enormous adj enor-mous: huge, vast
The *enormous* elephant couldn't fit into the cage.

enthrall v en-thrall: fascinate
Looking at New York City's skyscrapers *enthralls* tourists.

entice v en-tice: to tempt
Please don't *entice* me to have any more ice cream.

entomb v en-tomb: to bury
They found the mummy *entombed* on the other side of the hill.

enumerate v e-nu-mer-ate: to list, count
She can *enumerate* all of the state flowers.

enunciate v e-nun-ci-ate: pronounce clearly
She was able to *enunciate* every word even though she was eating.

environment n en-vi-ron-ment: surroundings
Camping is an enjoyable means of living in an outdoor *environment*.

envoy n en-voy: messenger
The *envoy* brought the flowers.

eon n e-on: long period of time
Many *eons* ago, dinosaurs roamed our continent.

epic n ep-ic: long poem
Tennyson's *epics* are romantic and sad.

epidemic n ep-i-dem-ic: widespread disease
The measles *epidemic* spread throughout the school.

epigram n ep-i-gram: a bright or witty thought, tersely expressed
Oscar Wilde is noted for his *epigrams*.

epilogue n ep-i-logue: concluding section
You'll have to wait until the *epilogue* to discover how the story turns out.

episode n ep-i-sode: an incident
After the last *episode*, she refused to walk alone.

epistle n e-pis-tle: letter
The *epistle* was sent by messenger to the Pope.

epitaph n ep-i-taph: tomb inscription
The *epitaph* on his grave states that he lived for fifty years.

epitome n e-pit-o-me: summary
He was the *epitome* of the well-dressed man.

equanimity n e-qua-nim-i-ty: calm temper, evenness of mind
Adversity could not disturb his *equanimity*.

equestrian adj e-ques-tri-an: of horses or riding, on horseback
Polo and fox hunting are both *equestrian* sports.

equilibrium n e-qui-lib-ri-um: balance
After twirling around and around, the boy tried to regain his *equilibrium*.

equitable adj eq-ui-ta-ble: just, fair
The opponents came to an *equitable* settlement.

equivocal adj equiv-o-cal: uncertain, ambiguous
The *equivocal* statements left us in doubt as to his real intentions.

eradicate v e-rad-i-cate: to destroy
Smother the fire to *eradicate* it.

erode v e-rode: wear away
The ground was *eroded* by the wind and rain.

erratic adj er-rat-ic: irregular
As the car drove along the beach, it left an *erratic* pattern in the sand.

erratic n er-rat-ic: an erratic person
People call him an *erratic* because he changes his plans often.

erroneous adj er-ro-ne-ous: mistaken
His statement was *erroneous* and had nothing to do with the conversation.

erudite adj er-u-dite: scholarly, learned
He was *erudite* without being stuffy.

erupt v e-rupt: to break out
The volcano *erupted* streams of lava.

escalate v es-ca-late: increase
The war *escalated* and more troops were brought in.

escapade n es-ca-pade: adventure
When the boys returned from their *escapade* they were dirty and tired.

eschew v es-chew: to avoid
I would like to *eschew* that topic, if possible.

esoteric adj es-o-ter-ic: limited to a few, secret
The *esoteric* rites of the fraternity were held sacred by the members.

espouse v es-pouse: to marry
They were *espoused* after the party.

esteem v es-teem: to value highly
She was *esteemed* for her ability to deal with difficult situations.

esteem n es-teem: high regard
The boy had great *esteem* for his father.

estuary n es-tu-ar-y: part of a river that meets the sea
The ship was caught in the currents of the *estuary* when the tides were going in.

eternal adj e-ter-nal: everlasting
As long as there are wars, there will not be *eternal* peace in the world.

ethereal adj e-the-re-al: delicate, airy, light
She looked *ethereal* as she walked into the room.

ethics n eth-ics: moral conduct
The judge had the highest *ethics* and was well respected.

ethnic adj eth-nic: belonging to the customs of a national group
Of all the *ethnic* foods available in this city, Italian pizza is the most popular.

etiquette n et-i-quette: rules of behavior
It is considered good *etiquette* to say 'thank you' when you receive a present from another person.

eulogy n eu-lo-gy: praising speech
The *eulogy* delivered at the funeral expressed all of our sentiments.

euphonic adj eu-pho-nic: pleasant-sounding
Her *euphonic* singing had a soothing effect on the guests.

euphoria n eu-pho-ri-a: sense of well-being
They went through a period of *euphoria* after winning the lottery.

evacuate v e-vac-u-ate: to leave, withdraw, to make empty
The soldiers *evacuated* the town.

evade v e-vade: avoid
He *evaded* the police's questioning.

evict v e-vict: to expel, force out
The tenants were *evicted* from his apartment.

evince v e-vince: to make evident, display
His curt reply *evinced* his short temper.

eviscerate v e-vis-cer-ate: to desembowel
Animals must be *eviscerated* before they can be cooked or smoked.

evoke v e-voke: to bring out
The photograph *evoked* memories of an earlier time.

evolve v e-volve: to develop slowly
These trees have *evolved* from an earlier form of bush.

ewe n ewe: female sheep
They gathered the *ewes* and their babies for feeding.

exaggerate v ex-ag-ger-ate: overstate
Andrew *exaggerated* the strength and size of his older brother.

exalt v ex-alt: to glorify, honor
The King was *exalted* by his subjects.

exasperate v ex-as-per-ate: to vex, irritate
Those loud noises are *exasperating* to the man trying to sleep.

excavate v ex-ca-vate: to dig, make hollow
The men *excavated* the site to prepare for the new building.

excessive adj ex-ces-sive: too much
Excessive sun will cause sunburn.

exclaim v ex-claim: say, speak
He *exclaimed* that he was very surprised.

excursion n ex-cur-sion: journey
The *excursion* lasted a whole day.

execute v ex-e-cute: to carry out; to kill
He was unable to *execute* the orders.
The prisoner was *executed* at dawn.

exert v ex-ert: to put into action
He physically *exerted* himself as he mowed the lawn.

exhort v ex-hort: to urge
They continued to *exhort* the troops forward.

exhume v ex-hume: to dig out, disinter
He obtained a court order to *exhume* the body.

exile n ex-ile: banishment
They had to leave their country for *exile*.

exile v ex-ile: to banish
The prince was *exiled* from his country because of his bad behavior.

existence n ex-is-tence: life, being
Some people believe that the *existence* of the world began with a spark.

exodus n ex-o-dus: departure
Cold weather caused the *exodus* of the birds to warmer climates.

exonerate v ex-on-er-ate: to free from blame
The man was *exonerated* of the charges.

exorbitant adj ex-or-bi-tant: excessive
That store charges *exorbitant* prices.

exorcise v ex-or-cise: to drive out, free from
The men tried to *exorcise* the devil by praying over the child.

exotic adj ex-ot-ic: foreign, strange
The *exotic* belly dancers performed in the restaurant.

expedite v ex-pe-dite: to speed up
If you sign this form, it will *expedite* matters.
expel v ex-pel: to force out
The boy was *expelled* from class.
experiment n ex-per-i-ment: test, trial
The *experiment* using rats continued in the lab.
experiment v ex-per-i-ment: to try or test something
He *experimented* with different designs until he was satisfied.
expire v ex-pire: to end; die
Remember to renew your license before it *expires*.
The patient *expired* at one o'clock.
explicit adj ex-pli-cit: definite, clear
Be *explicit* in giving directions to your house so that we will have
no trouble finding it.
exploit n ex-ploit: daring deed
The *exploits* of astronauts are applauded by the world.
exploit v ex-ploit: to promote, publicize
The agency tried to *exploit* the healthy aspects of the product.
expressly adv ex-press-ly: specifically
I wrote it *expressly* for you.
expurgate v ex-pur-gate: to remove objectionable matter
The censors *expurgated* the portions of the book they considered
obscene.
exquisite adj ex-qui-site: delicate, lovely
She owned an *exquisite* pearl necklace.
extensive adj ex-ten-sive: broad, wide
The coverage of the news team was *extensive*.
extinguish v ex-tin-guish: to put out (like a fire)
The water *extinguished* the fire.
extol v ex-tol: to praise highly
The teacher *extolled* the pupil's skill.
extract v ex-tract: pull out
The dentist will have to *extract* that bad tooth.
exult v ex-ult: to rejoice
The winner *exulted* in his victory.

F

fable n fa-ble: story
The *fable* about "Peter Pan" is a favorite with children.
fabricate v fab-ri-cate: construct
On this hill, they plan to *fabricate* a log house.
facetious adj fa-ce-tious: joking
I was only being *facetious* and didn't mean what I said.
facsimile n fac-sim-i-le: a reproduction, copy
That is a *facsimile* of a Picasso painting.
fad n fad: craze, rage
The mini-skirt *fad* seems to be popular again.
faint adj faint: feeble, languid, exhausted
The children were *faint* with fatigue and hunger.
fallacy n fal-la-cy: false or deceiving ideas
His reasoning was filled with *fallacies*.
fallow adj fal-low: uncultivated, inactive
The farmer's field lay *fallow* for a year.
falter v fal-ter: to hesitate, stumble
He began to *falter* as he approached the throne.
famine n fam-ine: starvation
 Famine ravaged the countryside and left the people hungry.
fanatic adj fa-nat-ic: characterized by an extreme viewpoint
Some credos seem to create *fanatic* followers among the discontented.
fantasy n fan-ta-sy: imagination
Her dreams were full of *fantasy*.
fastidious adj fas-tid-i-ous: hard to please
He was a *fastidious* person and found fault with almost everything.
fatal adj fat-al: deadly
The bullet shot was *fatal*.
fathom n fath-om: a measure of length used chiefly at sea
The water was twenty *fathoms* deep.
fatigue n fa-tigue: weariness
The *fatigue* continued until he found time to rest.
fawn n fawn: young deer
A *fawn* is one of the animals in the zoo's nursery.
feasible adj fea-si-ble: capable, able
That is a *feasible* suggestion, and we will try it.

feeble adj fee-ble: weak
 After her illness, her legs were *feeble*.
feign v feign: pretend
 She tried to *feign* illness to avoid going to the party.
felicity n fe-lic-i-ty: happiness
 Felicity was felt by all when the couple married.
feline adj fe-line: cat family
 Although lions and tigers are different animals, they belong to the same *feline* category.
felonious adj fe-lo-nious: criminial
 He was charged with a *felonious* act.
ferocious adj fe-ro-cious: cruel, fierce
 He owned a *ferocious* dog.
fetch v fetch: to bring
 If you throw it, the dog will *fetch* the ball.
fetid adj fet-id: bad smelling
 The meat was *fetid* and had to be thrown out.
fetus n fe-tus: unborn animal in the womb
 Damage to the *fetus* may be caused by any shock to a pregnant female.
feud n feud: quarrel
 The *feud* between the two families has gone on for many years.
feud v feud: to carry on a feud
 The boys *feuded* with each other over use of the bicycle.
fiasco n fi-as-co: a ridiculous failure
 The play was a *fiasco* and closed the next day.
fickle adj fick-le: changing
 She is a *fickle* person because she is always changing her mind.
fictitious adj fic-ti-tious: imaginary, assumed
 The story is *fictitious* but seems so real.
fidelity n fi-del-i-ty: loyalty
 You can appreciate his *fidelity* but not his stubbornness.
fidget v fid-get: to be uneasy or restless
 He *fidgeted* in his seat while the lecture continued.
fiend n fiend: evil spirit, demon
 He ate like a *fiend*, as though he were possessed.
figurine n fig-u-rine: statue, sculpture
 The *figurine* stood on a tall pedestal.
finagle v fi-na-gle: to cheat
 The students were caught *finagling* on the exam.
finesse n fi-nesse: skill
 He is considered the best mechanic in town because of his *finesse* in repairing cars.

finicky adj fin-ick-y: fussy
The child's eating habits were *finicky* and he only enjoyed soft foods.
finite adj fi-nite: having a limit, bounded
There was only a *finite* number of men to be considered for the job.
fiscal adj fis-cal: financial
This is the end of the *fiscal* year.

fission n fis-sion: splitting
The *fission* of the molecules was something he had been trying to achieve for many years.
flabbergast v flab-ber-gast: to amaze, to astound
He was *flabbergasted* when he saw how well she danced.
flaccid adj flac-cid: limp, weak
His hand was *flaccid* and unpleasant to shake.

flagrant adj fla-grant: outrageous
Be careful that your *flagrant* behavior does not get you into trouble.
flair n flair: talent
He had a *flair* for dressing nicely.
flamboyant adj flam-boy-ant: ornate, brilliant
More people will notice your passing by if you wear that *flamboyant* outfit.
flask n flask: container, bottle
He kept the wine in a silver *flask*.
flaunt v flaunt: show off
She *flaunted* her new dress at the party.

flaw n flaw: defect, crack
The *flaw* in the material was hardly evident.
flee v flee: to run away
They tried to *flee* from the police after the robbery.
fleece v fleece: to rob, to shear the wool from
The man tried to *fleece* the couple out of their money.
It is necessary to *fleece* sheep in the spring.
flexible adj flex-ible: easily bent, adaptable
The plastic was *flexible* when heated and could be molded into the desired shape.
flimflam v flim-flam: to cheat, to trick
He was well-known for trying to *flimflam* older couples.
flimsy adj flim-sy: frail, thin
The *flimsy* nightgown revealed her body.
flinch v flinch: to pull back from
He *flinched* every time the bee flew by him.
flock n flock: group, crowd
The farmer herded a *flock* of sheep away from the pond.

flog v flog: whip
The captain had the sailor *flogged* in front of the others.

flotilla n flo-til-la: fleet of ships
Their boat was in the middle of the *flotilla*.

flotsam n flot-sam: floating wreckage
The water was covered with *flotsam* from the sunken liner.

flounder v floun-der: to struggle
The boy was *floundering* in the heavy waves.

flounder n floun-der: type of flat fish
He enjoyed eating his *flounder* with lemon and butter.

flourish v flour-ish: to do well
The neighborhood began to *flourish* after the road was built.

flourish n flour-ish: something done in a showy way
She twirled the baton with a *flourish* to begin the parade.

fluctuate v fluc-tu-ate: to change, vary
She *fluctuated* in her moods and we never knew what she would do next.

flue n flue: chimney pipe
When he lit a fire in the fireplace, smoke rose up out of the *flue*.

flume n flume: a narrow water channel, often artificial
They diverted the water into a *flume* for sending the logs down the side of the mountain.

flurry n flur-ry: sudden gust
It was a *flurry* of leaves that blinded him momentarily.

flush v flush: to blush
She began to *flush* from the heat.

flush n flush: a rapid going, as of water
The *flush* of water cleaned the tea kettle.

flush adj flush: well-supplied
He returned from town, *flush* with food and drink.

fluster v flus-ter: to confuse
The girl was *flustered* by all the attention.

fodder n fod-der: food for cattle
The truck delivered the pig *fodder* in the morning.

foe n foe: enemy
They were *foes* on the baseball diamond, but friends afterwards.

foible n foi-ble: weakness
His *foible* was that he was often shy and private.

foliage n fo-li-age: leaves
The *foliage* is most colorful during the Fall.

fondle v fon-dle: to caress
She began to *fondle* her daughter's hair.

foray n for-ay: plundering raid
    The bandits made a *foray* into town.
forestall v fore-stall: to prevent, hold off
    You can only *forestall* the battle for a little while.
foretell v fore-tell: to predict
    I can *foretell* the outcome of the game.
forfeit v for-feit: to give up
    He had decided to *forfeit* his comfortable life for the sea.
forfeit n for-feit: fine, penalty for fault or crime
    He was required to pay a *forfeit* when he lost the game.
forlorn adj for-lorn: neglected, unhappy
    The *forlorn* cat sat in the corner, staring at the boy.
format n for-mat: plan, arrangment
    He liked the *format* of the book he was reading.
fortify v for-ti-fy: strengthen
    The sailors *fortified* their position by erecting a wall.
fossil n fos-sil: remains
    The *fossil* of the jaw was found in the tar pit.
fowl n fowl: a type of bird
    He ate a balanced diet of fish, meat, and *fowl*.
foyer n foy-er: entrance hall
    They entered the living room from the *foyer*.
fracas n fra-cas: brawl, quarrel
    They were both bloody from the *fracas*.
fragile adj frag-ile: easily broken
    The antique vase was *fragile* and was always kept on a high shelf.
fragrance n fra-grance: scent, odor
    The sweet *fragrance* of lilacs filled the room.
frail adj frail: weak
    She was tiny and *frail* and frightened of the world.
franchise n fran-chise: right to vote
    Your *franchise* allows you the chance to support your favorite candidate for office.
frantic adj fran-tic: excited
    The squirrel was *frantic* in his search for the acorn.
friction n fric-tion: irritation caused by rubbing; clash of opinions
    The *friction* of the rough cloth on his arm caused an infection.
    There was *friction* in the office.
fringe n fringe: border, trimming, the edge
    There was a lace *fringe* on the tablecloth.
    He was friends with the radical *fringe*.

frivolous adj friv-o-lous: silly, foolish
   She was completely *frivolous*, with no serious thoughts.
frock n frock: dress, gown
   She wore a simple *frock* made by her mother.
froth v froth: to foam, bubble
   The sick dog began to *froth* at the mouth.
froth n froth: foam
   The *froth* on top of a malted is the best part.
frugal adj fru-gal: thrifty
   They were both *frugal* and able to save a lot of money.
frustrate v frus-trate: to thwart
   He was *frustrated* in his attempt to get elected.
furnish v furn-ish: supply, provide
   He *furnished* the troops with additional guns.
furtive adj fur-tive: secret
   His *furtive* movements made him a likely suspect.
fuse v fuse: unite, blend
   He was able to *fuse* the ends of the rope together.
futile adj fu-tile: useless, trivial
   The search was *futile*, and the helicopters returned to their base.

G

gadget n gad-get: device
   This new house is filled with interesting *gadgets*.
gainsay v gain-say: to deny
   It was impossible to *gainsay* the truth of the statement the man made.
gale n gale: strong wind
   The *gale* blew down most of the palm trees.
gallant adj gal-lant: stately, grand
   His *gallant* stance showed everyone how proud he was.
gape v gape: open wide
   Her eyes *gaped* like huge saucepans as she saw him come near.
garb n garb: clothing
   She wore the latest *garb* to the party.
garb v garb: to dress, clothe
   He was *garbed* in his father's suit.

garish adj gar-ish: flashy
Everyone noticed her *garish* clothes.

garland n gar-land: a wreath
They hung a *garland* of flowers on the winning horse.

garnish v gar-nish: to decorate
They *garnished* the wedding cake with chocolate.

garnish n gar-nish: a decoration
She used the flower as a *garnish* for the dessert.

garrulous adj gar-ru-lous: talkative
The play was *garrulous* and bored most of the viewers.

gash n gash: deep cut
She poured antiseptic on the *gash* to prevent infection.

gash v gash: to make a long, deep cut
He *gashed* the bark of the tree to mark the path.

gaudy adj gau-dy: showy and cheap, flashy
Her make-up was *gaudy* and made her look ridiculous.

gauge n gauge: a standard measure
You can determine the *gauge* of the tire by measuring it.

gauge v gauge: to measure the size, amount, etc.
Gauge your distance from the curb before you park the car.

gaunt adj gaunt: thin
Her hands seemed *gaunt* in the tight-fitting gloves.

gauntlet n gaunt-let: glove
The hawk rested on the leather *gauntlet* before he took off in flight.

gawky adj gawk-y: clumsy
The teenager was *gawky* and knocked down everything.

gazette n ga-zette: newspaper
He read the story in the local *gazette*.

generate v gen-er-ate: produce
Pianos *generate* beautiful sound if you strike the right keys.

genesis n gen-e-sis: origin, creation
The *genesis* of his idea began during a dinner conversation.

genial adj gen-ial: pleasant
She was a *genial* hostess.

genteel adj gen-teel: polite, well-bred
People liked her *genteel* manner.

germane adj ger-mane: relevant
The topic was *germane* to the discussion.

gist n gist: main idea
He got the *gist* of it when he finished the book.

glaucoma n glau-co-ma: eye disease
He suffered from *glaucoma* and needed an operation.

glean v glean: gather
Glean as much information as you can before you start writing your
book.

glee n glee: great joy, merriment
He shouted with *glee* when he found the money.

gloss n gloss: shiny covering
The floor was buffed to a high *gloss*.

gloss v gloss: pass over quickly
He tried to *gloss* over the real reason he had come.

glut v glut: to fill fully
He *glutted* himself as he continued to eat and drink.

glutton n glut-ton: overeater
He was a *glutton* at the table.

gnash v gnash: to grind
The animal *gnashed* his teeth as he ate.

gnome n gnome: dwarf
The Grimm Brothers wrote about *gnomes* and elves.

goad v goad: to urge on
He was *goaded* by his parents to finish the project.

goblet n gob-let: drinking glass
They served the water in crystal *goblets*.

gorge n gorge: valley
The *gorge* was flooded with water.

gorge v gorge: eat greedily
He *gorged* himself on candy and cookies.

gory adj gor-y: bloody
Don't tell me the *gory* details of the murder.

govern v gov-ern: to rule, control
He was unable to *govern* his country.

gracious adj grac-ious: pleasant
The young, *gracious* girl was escorted to her table.

grapple v grap-ple: to seize, lay fast hold on
He *grappled* with the man who had attacked him.

grasp v grasp: to seize, hold on to
She *grasped* his hand for safety.

grasp n grasp: a grip; an understanding
Her *grasp* of the subject was amazing.
The man shook hands with a firm *grasp*.

gratis adv gra-tis: free of charge
The meal was presented *gratis* by the management.

gratuity n gra-tu-i-ty: tip
He left a *gratuity* for the chambermaid.

grave n grave: hole in the ground to bury the dead
The *grave* was freshly dug and prepared for the deceased.

grave adj grave: serious
He made a *grave* error when he stole the car.

grieve v grieve: to be very sad
He *grieved* over the loss of his wife.

grim adj grim: cruel, stern
His face was *grim* and frightening.

grimace n grim-ace: ugly, funny smile
His *grimace* gave a peculiar look to his face.

grimace v grim-ace: to make grimaces
She *grimaces* at her reflection in the mirror.

grimy adj grim-y: very dirty
The child's *grimy* hands were from playing outdoors.

grind v grind: to crush
You can watch them *grind* the coffee beans into powder.

grope v grope: search blindly
She *groped* around in the dark, looking for the light switch.

grotesque adj gro-tesque: odd, ugly
Witches are noted for their *grotesque* noses.

grotto n grot-to: a cave
The *grotto* was damp and filled with bats.

grouse v grouse: to complain
There is no use *grousing* over your own mistakes.

grovel v grov-el: to humble oneself
He was forced to *grovel* in order to be fed.

grudge n grudge: ill will
I hold no *grudge* against you.

grudge v grudge: to give reluctantly
He *grudged* his son even the priviledge of driving the family's car.

grueling adj gru-el-ing: exhausting
The labor was so *grueling* that two workers fainted.

gruesome adj grue-some: horrible
The Halloween mask of the monster was *gruesome*.

gruff adj gruff: rough
His manner was so *gruff* that most of the children feared him.

guffaw v guf-faw: to laugh loudly
The man *guffawed* when the child did a flip.

guile n guile: craftiness, deceit
Don't practice your *guile* on me.

gullible adj gul-li-ble: easily cheated
It is easy to take advantage of *gullible* people.

gush v gush: pour out
The water *gushed* out of the ground.

gust n gust: rush of wind
The *gust* blew his hat off his head.

guzzle v guz-zle: to drink much, to drink frequently
He *guzzled* his liquor like a man dying of thirst.

gyrate v gy-rate: to rotate
The dancers on the floor *gyrated* to the music.

H

haberdashery n hab-er-dash-er-y: men's clothing
His *haberdashery* was the latest style.

hack v hack: to chop
He was able to *hack* down the branches.

hackneyed adj hack-neyed: commonplace, ordinary
He used a *hackneyed* expression that everyone knew.

haggle v hag-gle: to bargain
The old woman *haggled* for an hour about the price.

hail v hail: to greet
He *hailed* his friend from the other side of the street.

hail n hail: precipitation in the form of ice lumps
The *hail* began to fall, sounding like cannons firing.

hallucination n hal-lu-ci-na-tion: false vision
She was awakened by *hallucinations* in the middle of the night.

hamlet n ham-let: village
He lived in a little *hamlet* alongside the river.

handicap n hand-i-cap: hinderance; contest with assigned difficulty
She did not consider her blindness a *handicap*.
He played golf with a four-stroke *handicap*.

haphazard adj hap-haz-ard: random
He was hit by the *haphazard* throw.

hapless adj hap-less: unlucky
After a *hapless* day hunting, he came home and went to sleep.

harass v ha-rass: to annoy, worry
The dog began to *harass* the children.

hardy adj har-dy: strong, capable
He was a *hardy* fellow, able to lift the logs easily.

harpoon n har-poon: spear, used in whaling
The *harpoon* was thrown from the deck of the ship.

harpoon v har-poon: to strike with a spear or harpoon
The whale was *harpooned* by the sailor.

harsh adj harsh: strong, rough
She couldn't stand the *harsh* winters of Alaska.

hassle n has-sle: struggle
It was a *hassle* trying to rent a car.

haste n haste: quickness
In his *haste* he tripped over the bush.

haughty adj haugh-ty: proud, insolent
Because of his new job, he was *haughty*.

haul v haul: to transport by wagon, truck, etc.
They planned to *haul* the dirt to his house.

haven n ha-ven: safe shelter
The boat pulled into the *haven* with the others.

havoc n hav-oc: chaos, ruin
The *havoc* was caused by the runaway bull.

hazardous adj haz-ard-ous: dangerous, risky
Although he was frightened, he volunteered for
the *hazardous* mission.

hazy adj ha-zy: misty, smoky
The sky was *hazy* from the pollution.

heap n heap: a pile
He found a *heap* of dirt in the yard.

heap v heap: to make into a pile
She *heaped* the vegetables onto his plate.

hearth n hearth: a fireplace
They sat around the open *hearth*, warming their hands.

heathen n hea-then: non-believer
He considered himself to be a *heathen*, compared to his friends.

heave v heave: to lift
They *heaved* the package to the second floor window.

heckle v heck-le: to annoy, bother
They began to *heckle* the speaker from the audience.

heinous adj hei-nous: hateful, offensive
He committed a *heinous* crime.

hence adv hence: thus, therefore
I am tired, *hence* I won't go with you.

heresy n her-e-sy: unaccepted belief
His book attacked the group's *heresy*.

hex n hex: magic spell
The roof on the barn had a *hex* symbol painted on it.
hiatus n hi-a-tus: space where something is missing
There was a long *hiatus* in the conversation, and then he began speaking again.
hibernate v hi-ber-nate: to sleep
The bear crawled into its cave to *hibernate* for the winter.
hideous adj hid-e-ous: extremely ugly
She wore a *hideous* fright mask to the party.
hieroglyphics n hi-er-o-glyph-ics: symbolic pictures
They found the ancient *hieroglyphics* painted on the walls of the cave.
hindrance n hin-drance: obstacle
The rock in the road is a *hindrance* to motorists trying to pass by in their cars.
hint n hint: suggestion
Give me a little *hint* about the present.
hint v hint: to intimate
She *hinted* at a new project she might begin.
hoard v hoard: to save, store away
He wanted to *hoard* all of the gold for himself.
hoard n hoard: a stored supply
We found his private *hoard* of food in the cave.
hoax n hoax: trick
He was fooled by the children's hoax.
hoax v hoax: to deceive with a trick
She was *hoaxed* into believing he would be there.
hobble v hob-ble: to limp
After the game, he had to *hobble* home.
hoist v hoist: to lift up
He tried to *hoist* the box on his back.
hoist n hoist: machine for lifting
The huge *hoist* was able to unload the car from the hold of the boat.
holocaust n ho-lo-caust: destruction by fire
After the *holocaust*, there were no buildings left standing.
homage n hom-age: honor, respect
They paid *homage* to the retired general.
homely adj home-ly: ugly, plain looking
She was a pleasant but *homely* child.
homicide n hom-i-cide: killing
The man was accused of *homicide* by the police.
homogeneous adj ho-mo-ge-ne-ous: similar
It was a *homogeneous* group of people that came to the lecture.

hone v hone: to sharpen
He *honed* his knife on the stone.
horde n horde: crowd
The *horde* of bees made us leave the picnic.
hormone n hor-mone: organic fluid that affects certain cells
Our bodies respond to changes in *hormone* levels.
hose n hose: stockings
Be careful that you don't get a run in your *hose*.
hose v hose: to water
If she *hoses* the garden, the flowers will grow faster.
hostile adj hos-tile: unfriendly
The neighbors were *hostile* to the new family.
hover v hov-er: to stay close to
The bird *hovered* above the water, watching for bugs.
humane adj hu-mane: merciful, kind
It was an *humane* act to take in the stray cat.
humbug n hum-bug: fraud
His plan was pure *humbug*.
humdrum adj hum-drum: boring, commonplace
It was a very *humdrum* job, so he quit.
humid adj hu-mid: damp
The air was so *humid* that my clothes were wet.
humiliate v hu-mil-i-ate: to embarrass
She was *humiliated* in front of her family.
hurdle n hur-dle: barrier, obstacle
The *hurdle* in the road prevented the cars from going any further.
hurdle v hur-dle: to jump over, to overcome
The runner *hurdled* the puddles.
hygienic adj hy-gi-en-ic: sanitary, healthful
Keep the sick patients in *hygienic* rooms.
hypocrite n hyp-o-crite: one who pretends to be something else, liar
Since you smoke, you are a *hypocrite* to tell me to stop.
hypothetical adj hy-po-thet-i-cal: assumed
Their plan to attack the building was only *hypothetical*.
hysterical adj hys-ter-i-cal: uncontrollable emotion, very excited
She became *hysterical* after the accident.

I

ideal adj i-de-al: standard of perfection
It was the *ideal* gift for his wife.
ideal n i-de-al: an idea of perfection
She was his *ideal* of the perfect woman.
idiom n id-i-om: expression common to a specific group
"Bury the hatchet," is a typical *idiom*, and means something other than what it says.
idle adj i-dle: not busy
When he was out of work, he was *idle* for almost a month.
idle v i-dle: to move slowly, waste time
They *idled* their way home from the movies.
ignoble adj ig-no-ble: low, base
It was an *ignoble* gesture, and they were embarrassed by him.
ignominious adj ig-no-min-i-ous: disgraceful
It was an *ignominious* defeat.
illuminate v il-lu-mi-natc: to light up
The tree was *illuminated* with a hundred bulbs.
illusory adj il-lu-so-ry: misleading
Because your report was *illusory*, I came to the wrong conclusion.
imbibe v im-bibe: to drink
The man continued to *imbibe* too much alcohol.
immense adj im-mense: huge
The aircraft carrier was *immense*.
immerse v im-merse: put into liquid
He *immersed* his head in the water to stop the pain.
imminent adj im-mi-nent: about to occur
His arrival is *imminent*.
immobile adj im-mo-bile: not movable
The rock was completely *immobile*, so they built around it.
immortal adj im-mor-tal: to live forever, without death
Shakespeare's plays are *immortal*.
immune adj im-mune: protected, safe
He was *immune* from measles because of the injection.
imp n imp: little devil, troublemaker
My son is an *imp*, but cute.
impair v im-pair: to damage
Too much loud noise may *impair* your hearing.

impale v im-pale: pierce
The animal was *impaled* on the spear.
impartial adj im-par-tial: fair
It was an *impartial* jury that made the decision.
impasse n im-passe: deadlock
They had reached an *impasse* in their negotiations.
impeccable adj im-pec-ca-ble: flawless, without fault
He was an *impeccable* dresser.
impel v im-pel: to force
They tried to *impel* him to tell the truth.
imperative adj im-per-a-tive: urgent, necessary
It is absolutely *imperative* that you call home.
impetus n im-pe-tus: incentive
The bonus is enough *impetus* to get me to finish the job.
implicate v im-pli-cate: to involve
He tried to *implicate* him in the robbery.
implore v im-plore: beg, plead with
The child *implored* her mother to let her stay up longer.
imply v im-ply: to suggest
He tried to *imply* that he was guilty.
inane adj in-ane: silly
It was an *inane* game they were planning.
inanimate adj in-an-i-mate: without life
He enjoyed painting *inanimate* objects rather than people.
incarcerate v in-car-cer-ate: to imprison
He was *incarcerated* for five years.
incense v in-cense: to make angry
He was *incensed* by his friend's statement.
incense n in-cense: substance producing fragrant odor when
burned
The children lit the *incense* in the bedroom.
incentive n in-cen-tive: motive, goal
I will offer you more money as an *incentive* to finish the project
early.
inception n in-cep-tion: beginning
At the *inception* of the project, he tried to resign.
incessant adj in-ces-sant: continuous
The *incessant* barking of the dog is getting me angry.
incident n in-ci-dent: happening, event
I remember the *incident* of the missing ring.
incinerate v in-cin-er-ate: to burn to ashes
He *incinerated* the secret papers.

incision n in-ci-sion: cut
The doctor made an *incision* along his ribs.
incite v in-cite: to arouse, stir up
The speaker began to *incite* the crowd to violence.
inclement adj in-cle-ment: stormy, rough
During *inclement* weather, be sure to carry an umbrella.
inclination n in-cli-na-tion: tendency
His *inclination* was to go home early.
incognito adv in-cog-ni-to: disguised
The movie star went to the party incognito.
incoherent adj in-co-her-ent: rambling, confused
After drinking too much, her speech was *incoherent*.
incredulous adj in-cred-u-lous: unbelieving, doubting
I am absolutely *incredulous* that you found that job.
increment n in-cre-ment: gradual increase
He filled the glass in *increments* of different colored liquids.
indefinite adj in-def-i-nite: not clear
I don't like it when you are *indefinite* about our plans.
indelible adj in-del-i-ble: permanent
He dripped *indelible* ink on his shirt.
index n in-dex: a list
He consulted the *index* at the back of the book.
index v in-dex: to categorize items
He started to *index* his coin collection.
indict v in-dict: to charge with an offense
The judge *indicted* him for assault.
indigo n in-di-go: blue dye
The natives harvested the *indigo* for sale to the traders.
induce v in-duce: to influence
He tried to *induce* the woman to buy his car.
induct v in-duct: install in office or military position
He was *inducted* into the army when he was eighteen.
inert adj in-ert: inactive
That machine will remain *inert* until you turn it on.
inevitable adj in-ev-i-ta-ble: unavoidable
It was *inevitable* that we would meet.
infallible adj in-fal-li-ble: without fail, reliable
I have an *infallible* system for memorizing names.
infamy n in-fa-my: disgrace, vile act
Custer's Last Stand will live in *infamy* forever.
infer v in-fer: conclude
From her tears, he was able to *infer* she was worried.

inferior adj in-fer-i-or: lower in rating
The workmanship in that coat is *inferior* to this one.
infinite adj in-fi-nite: without limits
The number of stars seems *infinite*.
infirm adj in-firm: weak, feeble
He was old and *infirm* and unable to attend the party.
inflate v in-flate: to puff out, swell
He *inflated* his son's balloon until it burst.
inflexible adj in-flex-ible: rigid, firm
The negotiator was *inflexible* in his demands.
inflict v in-flict: to give, cause
The soldier *inflicted* a bayonet thrust on the practice dummy.
influx n in-flux: flowing in
There was an *influx* of new people into the neighborhood.
inform v in-form: instruct, tell
Please *inform* the messenger where to deliver the package.
infraction n in-frac-tion: violation
You will be punished even for minor *infractions* of the rules.
infringe v in-fringe: to trespass, intrude
Try not to *infringe* on your brother's privacy.
infuriate v in-fu-ri-ate: to anger, enrage
His statements always *infuriate* me.
ingenious adj in-gen-ious: clever
It was the most *ingenious* solution to the problem.
ingredient n in-gre-di-ent: part of a mixture
He added another secret *ingredient* to the perfume.
inhabit v in-hab-it: to live in
The gophers *inhabited* those holes in the desert.
inhale v in-hale: to breathe
He *inhaled* the aroma of the cookies.
inherent adj in-her-ent: essential part of
This book is an *inherent* part of a reference library.
inhibit v in-hib-it: to restrict, restrain
I think it's necessary to *inhibit* your spending.
initiate v in-i-ti-ate: begin
He was the lawyer who *initiated* the defendant's lawsuit.
injunction n in-junc-tion: an order
She received an *injunction* against opening a business in town.
inkling n ink-ling: slight suggestion
She had an *inkling* there would be a party for her.
inn n inn: a small hotel
We stayed at a lovely, old country *inn*.

innate adj in-nate: natural
He had an *innate* sense of right and wrong.

innocuous adj in-nocu-ous: inoffensive, harmless
It seemed to be an *innocous* incident that angered him.

innovate adj in-no-vate: to introduce something new
He was known for his *innovative* painting techniques.

innuendo n in-nu-en-do: indirect suggestion
I'm tired of his *innuendos* about my work habits.

inordinant adj in-or-di-nate: too much, excessive
It was an *inordinant* amount of money to spend.

inquest n in-quest: legal inquiry
There was an *inquest* into the accident.

inquisitive adj in-quis-i-tive: questioning, curious
My children are all *inquisitive* about most things.

insane adj in-sane: crazy
He was judged to be *insane* and was sent to a hospital.

insight n in-sight: understanding, intuition
He had an *insight* into their problem and offered a solution.

insignia n in-sig-nia: badge, emblem
He wore his Captain's *insignia* on his hat.

insinuate v in-sin-u-ate: to hint at
She tried to *insinuate* that she had gone to the same party.

insipid adj in-sip-id: tasteless
It looks good, but has an *insipid* flavor.

insolent adj in-so-lent: rude, insulting
He was continually *insolent* to his teacher.

insolvent adj in-sol-vent: bankrupt
They cannot pay the rent in their *insolvent* state.

install v in-stall: to establish, put in
I will *install* the sink myself.

instigate v in-sti-gate: to stir up
She continued to *instigate* problems in the meeting.

instinct n in-stinct: a natural tendency
Birds fly south because of age-old *instincts*.

institute v in-sti-tute: to start, establish
He *instituted* a new plan to make the work flow faster.

institute n in-sti-tute: professional organization or place
He was elected to the head of the *institute*.

insurgent adj in-sur-gent: rebel
The *insurgent* troops came to the island by boat.

intact adj in-tact: untouched, uninjured
The train was surprisingly *intact* after the crash.

intangible adj in-tan-gi-ble: vague
He continues to make *intangible* demands.
integral adj in-te-gral: important, necessary
That cog is *integral* to the operation of the motor.
integrity n in-teg-ri-ty: honesty
His *integrity* could not be questioned.
intent n in-tent: purpose
It is my *intent* to complete the manuscript by tonight.
intent adj in-tent: firmly directed, earnest
His *intent* efforts quickly completed the job.
inter v in-ter: to bury
She was *interred* in the local cemetery.
interim n in-ter-im: intervening time, temporary
In the *interim* while the film is being shown, let's take a walk.
interject v in-ter-ject: to insert
I wish to *interject* my thoughts on that matter.
intermittent adj in-ter-mit-tent: recurrent
There was an *intermittent* siren from the firehouse.
interpret v in-ter-pret: to translate, explain
I am able to *interpret* these diagrams so they make sense.
interrogate v in-ter-ro-gate: to question
The prisoner was *interrogated* for three hours.
intervene v in-ter-vene: to come between
I had to *intervene* to stop the fight.
intimate adj in-ti-mate: familiar, personal
He is an *intimate* friend of mine.
intimate v in-ti-mate: to suggest, hint at
She *intimated* that she knew the secret already.
intimidate v in-tim-i-date: to frighten
He tried to *intimidate* the smaller children.
intolerable adj in-tol-er-able: unbearable
The heat was *intolerable*.
intoxicate v in-tox-i-cate: to make drunk
He was *intoxicated* after two drinks.
intrepid adj in-trep-id: fearless, bold
The *intrepid* leader of the troop marched into the combat zone.
intricate adj in-tri-cate: complicated
It was a very *intricate* mathematics problem.
intrigue n in-trigue: secret plot
They were caught up in political *intrigue*.
intrigue v in-trigue: to arouse the interest of
He was *intrigued* by her invitation to the dance.

invert v in-vert: reverse, turn upside down
He *inverted* the box over the frog.

invincible adj in-vin-ci-ble: unbeatable
The athlete was *invincible* at his own sport.

iota n i-o-ta: tiny quantity
I won't give you one *iota* of this money.

irate adj i-rate: angry
The *irate* customer demanded his money back.

ire n ire: anger
I think you are unreasonable in your *ire*.

irk v irk: to annoy
His habits always *irk* me.

irrigate v ir-ri-gate: supply water
It is necessary to *irrigate* the desert before those trees will grow.

irritable adj ir-ri-ta-ble: touchy
He was in a very *irritable* mood.

isolate v i-so-late: to place apart, separate
He was able to *isolate* the sick child from the others.

isthmus n isth-mus: connecting strip of land
Thousands of years ago, Alaska and Russia were connected by an *isthmus*.

iterate v it-er-ate: to repeat
He continued to *iterate* his story to the jury.

itinerant adj i-tin-er-ant: traveling
The *itinerant* salesman came to town again.

J

jab v jab: to poke
He continued to *jab* her in the back with his pencil.

jab n jab: a quick thrust or blow, a punch
The boxer had a strong left *jab*.

jackal n jack-al: African wild dog
The remains of the kill were finished off by the *jackals*.

jaded v jaded: dulled by excess
He was *jaded* by too much money.

jaunt n jaunt: short pleasure trip
I just came back from a European *jaunt*.

jaunty adj jaun-ty: happy, carefree
He walked with a *jaunty* step as he approached his girlfriend.

javelin n jav-e-lin: spear
He was the winner of the *javelin* throw.

jealous adj jeal-ous: envious
She was *jealous* of her sister's new clothes.

jeer v jeer: to make fun of, mock
The clown *jeered* at the crowd.

jeer n jeer: a jeering remark
The reporter's *jeer* about the man upset him.

jeopardy n jeop-ar-dy: danger
He was in constant *jeopardy* on the mountain climb.

jest n jest: a joke
He was not in the mood to be amused by her *jest*.

jest v jest: to joke, leer, banter
They continued to *jest* throughout the dinner.

jester n jest-er: a joker
He was a perpetual *jester*, never serious for a moment.

jettison v jet-ti-son: to throw overboard
They *jettisoned* the luggage to lighten the load.

jibe v jibe: to agree with
His story *jibes* with yours.

jinx n jinx: bad luck
She felt that her knife was a *jinx*, so she threw it away.

jocular adj joc-u-lar: funny, humorous
He was a *jocular* old man, loved by everyone.

jostle v jos-tle: to shove, push
She was *jostled* about in the train.

jovial adj jo-vi-al: merry, jolly
In his *jovial* way, the old man entertained the children.

jowl n jowl: jaw, cheek
The wolf dug his claws into the rabbit's *jowl*.

jubilant adj ju-bi-lant: rejoicing, happy
He was *jubilant* after winning the race.

judicious adj ju-di-cious: wise, well thought out
It was a *judicious* decision you made.

junction n junc-tion: place where things join
There was a leak at the *junction* of the two pipes.

junket n jun-ket: long trip, journey
They just returned from a European *junket*.

junta n jun-ta: group controlling government
The *junta* was now in charge of everything.

jury n ju-ry: a committee, appointed group
The *jury* voted him the first prize in the art contest.
justify v jus-ti-fy: to defend, prove to be right
I am able to *justify* my position on that matter.
jut v jut: to stick out
That tree *juts* out onto the sidewalk.
jut n jut: a part that juts
The *jut* in the road is causing traffic to reroute around it.
juvenile adj ju-ve-nile: young
It was a *juvenile* story.
juvenile n ju-ve-nile: a young person
He was considered a *juvenile* by the authorities.

K

keen adj keen: shrewd
He had a *keen* mind and grasped ideas quickly.
keg n keg: barrel, small cask
He brought a beer *keg* upstairs from the basement.
kelp n kelp: seaweed
In Japan, *kelp* is a basic part of the diet.
kettle n ket-tle: pot
She put the tea *kettle* on the stove.
kin n kin: family, close relatives
My closest *kin* live in Wisconsin.
kink n kink: twist, curl
You will not be able to use that wire with the *kink* in it.
kink v kink: to form or cause to form
Be careful not to *kink* the antenna out of shape.
kleptomania n klep-to-ma-ni-a: impulse to steal
They were concerned about their child's *kleptomania*.
knack n knack: ability, aptitude, skill
He had a *knack* for getting out of trouble.
knapsack n knap-sack: a backpack
She threw the *knapsack* across her back and marched away.
knave n knave: dishonest individual
He was a coward and a *knave*.

knead v knead: to mix, stir
It's important to *knead* the clay to get out air bubbles.
knell n knell: ringing of a bell
The happy *knell* was heard throughout the city.
knoll n knoll: small hill
It will be safe to let the children climb up the *knoll*.

L

labyrinth n lab-y-rinth: a maze
They were quickly lost in the dark *labyrinth*.
lacerate v lac-er-ate: tear roughly, mangle
The clothing was *lacerated* by the machine.
lackadaisical adj lack-a-dai-si-cal: listless
He was *lackadaisical* about finishing the job.
lackey n lack-ey: a servant
He was treated like a *lackey*, so he quit the job.
laconic adj la-con-ic: terse, brief
It was a *laconic* statement, but right to the point.
lacquer n lac-quer: varnish
He applied the *lacquer* over the old surface.
laden adj lad-en: loaded
The mules were *laden* with supplies for the trip.
lagoon n la-goon: a shallow pond
They went swimming in the nearby *lagoon*.
lair n lair: den, resting place
The animals were safe in their *lair*.
lament v la-ment: to mourn
I need time to *lament* the loss of my mother.
lament n la-ment: a crying out of grief
She could hear his sad *lament* in the other room.
lampoon n lam-poon: satire
The newspaper presented a *lampoon* about the party.
lampoon v lam-poon: to attack in a lampoon
The host *lampooned* the guest of honor in a witty speech.
lance n lance: a spear
The warriors carried *lances* to protect themselves.

lance v lance:　to pierce, cut
　The doctor *lanced* the infection.
lanquish v lan-guish:　to weaken
　He continued to *languish* as he lay in his bed.
languor n lan-guor:　weakness, indifference
　Because of his *languor*, no one wanted him on the team.
lanky adj lanky:　tall and thin
　The basketball player was *lanky* and nothing fit him.
lapse v lapse:　to slip
　He *lapsed* into his old speech pattern for a moment.

lapse n lapse:　a slight error
　It was a momentary *lapse*, but enough to cause the accident.
larceny n lar-ceny:　theft
　He committed *larceny* when he stole the car.
lard n lard:　fat
　They saved the bacon *lard* to make candles.
lard v lard:　to insert fat strips into meat before cooking
　The chef *larded* the roast before he put it into the oven.

lariat n lar-i-at:　lasso, rope
　The cowboy threw his *lariat* over the cow's head.
larva n lar-va:　insect egg
　The mosquito left its *larva* on a leaf.
latch n latch:　fastener
　Be sure to hook the *latch* on the door before you leave.
latch v latch:　to fasten with a latch
　Latch the windows tightly against the rain.
latent adj la-tent:　hidden
　Psychologists look for *latent* meanings behind what you say.
lather n lath-er:　foam
　He applied the *lather* to his face before shaving.
laud v laud:　to praise
　I must *laud* your recent performance in the play.
laurel n lau-rel:　wreath, praise, award
　He received the *laurels* for winning the race.
lava n la-va:　molten rock
　The *lava* poured from the mouth of the volcano.
lavish adj lav-ish:　abundant
　It was a *lavish* wedding with all of the trimmings.
lavish v lav-ish:　to give or spend abundantly
　He continued to *lavish* gifts upon his girlfriend.
lax adj lax:　loose, without discipline
　His *lax* control annoyed his employees.

lease n   lease: rental contract
She signed a new *lease* for her apartment.

lease v   lease: to rent
She was able to *lease* a car for a week.

lecherous adj   lech-er-ous: lewd, lustful
His *lecherous* remarks made him unwelcome at the party.

lecture n   lec-ture: a speech
They sat through his entire *lecture* without taking notes.

lecture v   lec-ture: to give a speech to
If you continue to *lecture* me, I will leave.

ledge n   ledge: shelf
I put the vase on the upper *ledge*.

ledger n   ledg-er: account book
The *ledger* contained all of their financial records.

leer n   leer: suggestive glance
He stood on the corner with a *leer* on his face.

legible adj   leg-i-ble: easily read
Her handwriting was extremely *legible*.

legion n   le-gion: soldiers, army
The Roman *Legion* came down from the hills.

legitimate adj   le-git-i-mate: lawful
He was the *legitimate* grandson of King Edward.

legume n   leg-ume: vegetable
The garden was filled with *legumes* and fruits.

leniency n   le-ni-en-cy: mildness, mercy
Since this was her first offense, her lawyer asked the judge for *leniency*.

leonine adj   le-o-nine: lionlike
His hair was a *leonine* mane, golden and shaggy.

lesion n   le-sion: injury, hurt, sore
He had a *lesion* on his arm that had to be treated.

lethal adj   le-thal: deadly
They gave the wolf a *lethal* dose of poison.

lethargic adj   leth-ar-gic: sluggish
After the operation, he was very *lethargic*.

lever n   lev-er: tool for prying or lifting
He used the *lever* to open the crate.

levitate v   lev-i-tate: to rise and float in air
The magician made her *levitate*, much to the pleasure of the crowd.

levity n   lev-i-ty: frivolity, lack of seriousness
His *levity* was out of place at the funeral.

levy v   lev-y: to impose upon (tax, fine, etc.)
The government *levied* high taxes on its citizens.

lewd adj lewd: not decent
 You will not be allowed in the restaurant in that *lewd* attire.
lexicon n lex-i-con: dictionary
 This *lexicon* will help you understand how to spell words.
liability n li-a-bil-i-ty: debt, something disadvantageous
 His financial *liabilities* were more than he could pay.

liaison n li-ai-son: connection, contact between groups
 She was the *liaison* between the White and Red teams.
liberate v lib-er-ate: to set free
 They were able to *liberate* the gold from the enemy troops.

limber adj lim-ber: flexible
 He was extremely *limber* for an older man.
limber v lim-ber: to make loose, flexible
 They began to *limber* up in exercise class.
limerick n lim-er-ick: short poem, usually five lines
 The children wrote a humorous *limerick* in class.
limp adj limp: without rigidity
 The *limp* piece of celery sat uneaten on his plate.

limp v limp: to walk with a lame leg
 He was able to *limp* across the room.
limp n limp: a halt or lameness in walking
 He had a very noticeable *limp* when he walked.
linger v lin-ger: to remain, stay on
 He continued to *linger* long after the game was over.
listless adj list-less: tired, without energy
 The hot, *listless* people sat around all day.

lithe adj lithe: supple, easily bent
 The gymnast had a *lithe* body.
litigation n lit-i-ga-tion: lawsuit
 The *litigation* will be presented in court.
loam n loam: fertile soil
 He had no trouble growing the flowers because of the *loam*.
loathe v loathe: to hate
 Children seem to *loathe* vegetables.
locust n lo-cust: migratory grasshopper
 The *locusts* descended upon the area, darkening the sky.
lodestone n lode-stone: magnet
 Columbus used a *lodestone* to navigate.
lofty adj loft-y: high, proud
 He had very *lofty* ideals and thought himself better than others.
logic n log-ic: science of reasoning
 His wise decision was based on his use of *logic*.

loiter v loi-ter: linger, hang around
The boys were *loitering* on the corner all evening.

loot n loot: stolen goods, spoils, plunder
They divided the *loot* among the three of them.

loot v loot: to plunder or steal
They were arrested for *looting* the bank.

lope v lope: to run
The dog *loped* across the field.

loquacious adj lo-qua-cious: extremely talkative
Once he had a few drinks, he became *loquacious*.

lubricate adj lub-ri-cate: make smooth with grease or oil
He *lubricated* the chain to make the bike go faster.

lucid adj lu-cid: clear
It was a *lucid* explanation, and I understood everything.

lucrative adj lu-cra-tive: profitable
His scheme proved to be very *lucrative*.

ludicrous adj lu-di-crous: ridiculous
That's a *ludicrous* statement.

lugubrious adj lu-gu-bri-ous: sad, dismal
He wore a *lugubrious* look on his face.

lull v lull: to calm, quiet
Lull the baby to sleep with soft music.

lull n lull: a short period of calm
The *lull* between the storms did not last long enough to dry the ground.

luminous adj lu-mi-nous: bright, shining
I can read the sign in the *luminous* reflection of the sunlight.

lunacy n lu-na-cy: insanity, craziness
That plan was absolute *lunacy*.

lunar adj lu-nar: related to the moon
Last night we saw the *lunar* eclipse.

lupine adj lu-pine: like a wolf
His *lupine* movements amazed his audience.

lurch v lurch: to move suddenly
Suddenly, the train *lurched* forward.

lurch n lurch: a difficult situation
She left him in the *lurch*, without any reason.

lure v lure: attract
He was able to *lure* people into his store.

lurid adj lu-rid: sensational, startling
Newspaper headlines announced the *lurid* story.

lurk v lurk: to stay out of sight
The man *lurked* in the bushes.

luscious adj lus-cious: delicious
She was overwhelmed by the *luscious* desserts.
lush adj lush: covered with abundant growth
The *lush* forest housed many different animals and birds.
lush n lush: a heavy drinker
He was the neighborhood *lush*.
lust n lust: strong desire, often sexual
He could not control his *lust* for her.
lustrous adj lus-trous: shining
Your hair is always *lustrous* after a shampoo.
lynx n lynx: wildcat
The *lynx* was surrounded by the dogs.
lyre n lyre: harp-like instrument
Classical music sometimes uses a *lyre* to add beautiful tones to music.

M

macabre adj ma-ca-bre: gruesome
The end of the movie was *macabre* and depressing.
maelstrom n mael-strom: whirlpool
The boat was caught in the unexpected *maelstrom*.
maestro n mae-stro: conductor
The *maestro* strode to the podium and raised his baton.
magistrate n mag-is-trate: government official, judge
They appeared before the *magistrate* to ask for more time.
magnanimous adj mag-nan-i-mous: generous
She was always *magnanimous* during holiday season.
magnify v mag-ni-fy: to enlarge
He tried to *magnify* his position in the firm to her, but she knew the truth.
magnitude n mag-ni-tude: size
The *magnitude* of your gift is overwhelming.
maim v maim: to cripple
He was almost *maimed* when the pipe fell on him.
maintain v main-tain: to keep, carry on
I want to *maintain* control of the company.

maize n maize: corn
Maize grew in the field.
maize adj maize: yellow
That blouse is a very pretty *maize* color.
majestically adv ma-jes-tical-ly: grand, noble
The trees stood *majestically* along the roads.
maladroit adj mal-a-droit: clumsy
His *maladroit* actions always got him into trouble.
malady n mal-a-dy: illness
She had a strange *malady*, and they couldn't discover a cure.
malediction n mal-e-dic-tion: a curse, oath
He cast a *malediction* upon his own family.
malicious adj ma-li-cious: show bad feelings, ill will
It was a *malicious* action, totally uncalled for.
malign v ma-lign: to slander
You *maligned* him for no reason.
malignant adj ma-lig-nant: evil, life-endangering disease
They found a *malignant* tumor when they operated on him.
mall n mall: promenade, public walk
She met him for lunch at the new shopping *mall*.
mallard n mal-lard: wild duck
A flock of *mallards* flew overhead.
malleable adj mal-le-a-ble: adaptable
The artist was able to use gold because it was so *malleable*.
mallet n mal-let: hammer
He used a wooden *mallet* to tap the shelf into place.
mammoth adj mam-moth: huge, gigantic
It was a *mammoth* wave that overturned the boats.
mammoth n mam-moth: extinct elephant with long tusks
They found the remains of the *mammoth* in the tar pits.
manacle n man-a-cle: handcuff
The *manacles* bit into his wrists.
manacle v man-a-cle: to put on handcuffs
The policeman *manacled* the prisoner's hands behind his back.
mandate n man-date: command, an order
She was given a *mandate* to change the entire office staff.
mandible n man-di-ble: jaw
The doctor had to operate on her lower *mandible*.
mangle v man-gle: to cut or tear roughly
The book was *mangled* by the broken machine.
mania n ma-ni-a: insanity, extreme enthusiasm
He had a *mania* for French wines.

manipulate v ma-nip-u-late: to operate skillfully
He was able to *manipulate* the pliers with ease.

manor n man-or: estate
He was the lord of the *manor*.

mansion n man-sion: regal residence
They lived in a *mansion*, surrounded by trees and streams.

manual adj man-u-al: accomplished by hand
He enjoyed *manual* labor.

manual n man-u-al: a book of instructions
He fixed the car, following the *manual* carefully.

manure n ma-nure: fertilizer
The lawn was covered with *manure*.

mar v mar: to spoil, damage
The wet glass *marred* the oak tabletop.

maraud v ma-raud: to raid, plunder
The jackals began to *maraud* through the hunter's camp.

margin n mar-gin: the border, edge
She wrote in the *margin* of her notebook.

marina n ma-ri-na: dock, wharf
He brought his boat into the *marina* for refueling.

marinate v mar-i-nate: to soak
The meat was *marinated* in the sauce to make it tender.

marionette n mar-i-o-nette: puppet
The *marionette* danced on its strings.

maroon v ma-roon: to leave abandoned
He was *marooned* on the island for a week.

maroon adj ma-roon: dark brownish red
He wore a *maroon* formal jacket.

marsh n marsh: swamp
He caught frogs in the *marsh*.

marsupial n mar-su-pi-al: group of lower mammals with external pouches.
Marsupials can be seen running free in Australia.

marsupial adj mar-su-pi-al: having characteristics of marsupials.
In this building is housed all the *marsupial* animals.

martial adj mar-tial: military
They were inspired by the *martial* music.

masonry n ma-son-ry: brickwork
He admired the *masonry* around the border of the house.

masquerade v mas-quer-ade: to disguise, dress up, pretend
He tried to *masquerade* as a doctor.

masquerade n mas-quer-ade: a costume party
She went to the *masquerade* dressed as a chef.

massacre n mas-sa-cre: wholesale killing, without mercy
Custer's Last Stand is an infamous *massacre*.

massacre v mas-sa-cre: slaughter
The buffalo were *massacred* by the hunters.

massive adj mas-sive: bulky, large
It was a *massive* box, big enough for an elephant.

masticate v mas-ti-cate: to chew
Please *masticate* the food thoroughly before swallowing.

matador n mat-a-dor: bullfighter
The *matador* entered the ring to wild cheers.

maternal adj ma-ter-nal: motherly
She showed her *maternal* feelings for the kitten.

mature adj mature: fully grown
The apples were not yet *mature*, so we couldn't pick them.

mature v ma-ture: to reach full development
She began to *mature* before her older brother.

mausoleum n mau-so-le-um: tomb
They found the *mausoleum* of the ancient Egyptian king.

maxim n max-im: proverb
My favorite *maxim* is "Do unto others…"

meager adj mea-ger: scanty
They ate a *meager* meal of cereal and water.

meander v me-an-der: to wander without purpose
They *meandered* slowly through the department store.

meddle v med-dle: interfere
Why do you *meddle* in everyone's business?

mediocre adj me-di-o-cre: average, ordinary
Although he is not the quickest worker, his work is certainly not *mediocre*.

meditate v med-i-tate: to think, contemplate
She wished to *meditate* on the problem for a while.

medium adj me-di-um: middle, moderate
He liked his steak done *medium* rare.

meek adj meek: mild-mannered, patient
He was much too *meek* to become a salesman.

megaphone n meg-a-phone: funnel-shaped horn for amplification
The cheerleaders shouted to the crowd through their *megaphones*.

melancholy n mel-an-choly: depression, gloom
He had sunk into a deep *melancholy*, and only his daughter could bring him out of it.

melee n me-lee: a wild, confused fight
The passersby were drawn into the *melee* without warning.
mellow adj mel-low: soft, calm
He was in a *mellow* mood.
melodius adj mel-o-di-us: sweet sounding
My daughter has a *melodius* singing voice.
memento n me-men-to: reminder
Please send a *memento* to each of the invited guests.
menace n men-ace: danger, threat
Wild animals can be a *menace* to the neighborhood.

menace v men-ace: to threaten
Those dark clouds are *menacing* the picnickers.
mend v mend: to repair, fix
She was not able to *mend* the torn dress herself.
mendacious adj men-da-cious: lying, untrue
It is a *mendacious* story.
mendicant n men-di-cant: beggar
The ragged *mendicant* came to our back door.

menial adj me-ni-al: degrading, low
He felt he was working in a *menial* job.
mentor n men-tor: teacher
He was my *mentor* in business.
mercenary n mer-ce-nary: hired soldier
The *mercenary* went to fight in Africa.

mercenary adj mer-ce-nary: done for money only
She was extremely *mercenary* and cared nothing for the people, only the money.
merchandise n mer-chan-dise: goods for sale
Let's see what *merchandise* that store supplies.
merchandise v mer-chan-dise: to buy or sell
Merchandise your pictures at the art fair.

merge v merge: to combine
Both roads *merged* at the top of the hill.
merit v mer-it: to deserve
I don't think he *merits* a raise in pay.

merit n mer-it: worth, value
I can better judge the *merit* of that film after seeing it again.
mesa n me-sa: plateau
In New Mexico, the highway runs between the *mesas*.
metamorphosis n met-a-mor-pho-sis: change of form
The *metamorphosis* of a caterpillar into a butterfly is interesting to watch.

metropolis n me-trop-o-lis: large city
New York is a major *metropolis* in the East.
microbe n mi-crobe: bacteria
They traced the illness to an air-borne *microbe*.
midget adj midg-et: miniature
He raced *midget* cars around the track.
migrate v mi-grate: to wander, travel
Every year the birds *migrate* south.
militant adj mil-i-tant: aggressive, fighting
A *militant* group of citizens gathered outside.
millennium n mil-len-ni-um: one thousand years
After the first *millennium*, life on earth began to develop.
mimic v mim-ic: to ape, imitate
She was able to *mimic* everything her mother did.
miniature adj min-i-a-ture: small, tiny
It was a *miniature* music box set into a watch.
miniature n min-i-a-ture: small painting or portrait
He was renown for his *miniatures* of noblemen.
minimal adj min-i-mal: least possible
Finish the work with *minimal* effort.
minion n min-ion: servant
He was surrounded by his *minions*.
minstrel n min-strel: poet or musician
The *minstrel* strolled through the garden.
mirage n mi-rage: an illusion
In the desert, the heat causes you to see *mirages* of waterholes.
mire n mire: soft, deep mud
The car was stuck in the *mire* in the meadow.
mire v mire: to cause to get stuck
The wheels were *mired* in the mud.
mirth n mirth: laughter, fun
He could hear the shouts of *mirth* coming from the room.
misanthrope n mis-an-thrope: hater of mankind
The town *misanthrope* lived alone on top of the hill.
mischievous adj mis-chie-vous: naughty
The kids were *mischievous*, but rarely were caught.
misdemeanor n mis-de-mean-or: small crime
Because his offense was considered a *misdemeanor*, the judge let him
go with just a warning.
miser n mi-ser: one who hoards money
He was a *miser*, and none of his children liked him.
mitigate v mit-i-gate: to lessen, soften
He tried to *mitigate* the blows from his father.

mobile adj mo-bile: able to be moved
They rented a *mobile* home for the summer.

mobile n mo-bile: sculptor's movable construction
Alexander Calder created famous *mobiles*; many of them hang in museums.

mock v mock: to laugh at, make fun of
He could only *mock* her appearance.

mock adj mock: false, imitation
The vegetarians serve *mock* hamburgers, actually made from vegetables.

modest adj mod-est: shy, bashful
She was extremely *modest* and didn't speak to many people.

modify v mod-i-fy: to change
I want to *modify* your computer to make it faster.

mogul n mo-gul: important executive
He was the image of the cigar-smoking movie *mogul*.

molar n mo-lar: a tooth
The dentist removed a loose *molar* from the boy's mouth.

molest v mo-lest: to annoy, bother
The man *molested* his co-workers.

mollify v mol-li-fy: to appease, soften
I tried to *mollify* him, but he was still angry.

molt v molt: to shed feathers
Birds *molt* at the end of the cold season.

momentous adj mo-men-tous: very important
The promotion was a *momentous* occasion for her.

monarch n mon-arch: ruler
He was the supreme *monarch* of all the countries.

mongrel n mon-grel: an animal or plant of mixed breed
The dog was cute, but he was only a *mongrel*.

monopoly n mo-nop-o-ly: total control
Their family had the local *monopoly* on vegetables.

monstrous adj mon-strous: enormous
The balloon was *monstrous* and held twenty people.

moratorium n mor-a-to-ri-um: legal delay
The crowd called for a *moratorium* in the arms race.

morbid adj mor-bid: unhealthy, diseased
He had a *morbid* fear of insects.

mores n mo-res: customs, rules
It's important to follow the local *mores* in order to fit in.

morose adj mo-rose: gloomy
After dinner, John grew *morose* and refused to talk.

morsel n mor-sel: small piece, fragment
There was only a *morsel* of food left on her plate.
mortician n mor-ti-cian: undertaker
The *mortician* was able to preserve the corpse for the police.
mortified v mor-ti-fied: ashamed, embarrassed
I am *mortified* by my error.
motto n mot-to: slogan
"The buck stops here" was President Truman's *motto*.
mucilage n mu-ci-lage: glue
The teacher attached the poster with *mucilage*.
muddle v mud-dle: to confuse, mix up, struggle with
He continued to *muddle* through the test.
muddle n mud-dle: a mess, confusion
They were caught in the middle of the *muddle*.
muffle v muf-fle: to cover up, wrap warmly
He was able to *muffle* the sounds by closing the door.
multitude n mul-ti-tude: crowd
His speech was attended by a *multitude* of friends.
mum adj mum: silent, without speech
I will keep *mum* on the subject of your brother.
mum n mum: a chrysanthemum
He brought her a bouquet of *mums*.
mundane adj mun-dane: worldly, common
Although he was a philosopher, his ideas were very *mundane*.
murky adj murk-y: dark, cloudy, gloomy
The cave was damp and *murky*, and we couldn't see.
murmur v mur-mur: to speak quietly
He tried to *murmur* in her ear during the party.
murmur n mur-mur: a low, continuous sound
The *murmur* of voices spread quickly through the room.
muster v mus-ter: to gather together
He tried to *muster* all of the horses together.
muster n mus-ter: an assembling
He called the men to *muster* in order to conduct an inspection.
mute adj mute: quiet, silent
The *mute* man learned sign language.
mute v mute: to soften
She tried to *mute* the noise with a pillow.
mutiny n mu-ti-ny: rebellion
The captain of the ship was overthrown by a *mutiny* of his sailors.
mutiny v mu-ti-ny: to revolt
The unhappy workers decided to *mutiny* against the boss.

myopic adj my-op-ic: near-sighted
She was extremely *myopic* and unable to see the screen.
myriad adj myr-i-ad: countless
He went through *myriad* nights without sleep.
myth n myth: legend, tale
I think that story is only a *myth* and not to be believed.

N

nadir n na-dir: lowest point
When he lost his job, he had reached the *nadir* of his career.
nag v nag: to irritate, annoy
Her mother *nagged* her to clean up her room.
nag n nag: the act of nagging; an inferior horse
Don't be such a *nag*.
The old *nag* finished last.
narrate v nar-rate: to tell, relate
She *narrated* the incident as she remembered it.
narrative adj nar-ra-tive: story, tale
His *narrative* speech delighted the audience.
narrative n nar-ra-tive: story form
Present your experience in a *narrative*.
nasal adj na-sal: pertaining to the nose
This *nasal* medicine may help clear up your breathing.
natal adj na-tal: birth
Come view the newborn infants in the *natal* department of the hospital.
naught n naught: nothing
Her efforts were for *naught* as no one appreciated her work.
nausea n nau-se-a: seasickness
A constant feeling of *nausea* spoiled her fun on the cruise.
nebulous adj neb-u-lous: cloudy, hazy, vague
It was a *nebulous* gesture and meant very little to anybody.
needy adj need-y: poor
The church is accepting donations for the *needy* survivors of the flood.
nefarious adj ne-far-i-ous: very wicked
He is disliked by many people because of his *nefarious* reputation.

neglectful adj ne-glect-ful: careless
Due to his *neglectful* use of the radio, it was ruined.

negligent adj neg-li-gent: careless
They won't entrust their boat to you if you treat it in a *negligent* manner.

negotiate v ne-go-ti-ate: arrange terms
They *negotiated* the contract between the teams.

neigh v neigh: to utter the characteristic cry of a horse
The horses *neighed* to their master from the barn.

nestle v nes-tle: settle
The cat *nestled* in the blanket.

neurotic n neu-rot-ic: emotionally unstable
Too many accidents have made her *neurotic* about driving.

neutral adj neu-tral: impartial, fair
The judge listened to the appeals with a *neutral* mind.

neutral n neu-tral: an impartial person or nation
A *neutral* will decide which of us is right.

nicety n ni-ce-ty: accuracy
He is a reliable accountant because of his *nicety* with figures.

niche n niche: a recess in a wall
The cat hid in a *niche*.

nigh adv nigh: almost
The report is *nigh* finished.

nil n nil: nothing
All their efforts were for *nil*.

nimble adj nim-ble: active
It took the efforts of two teachers to keep up with the *nimble* children.

nocturnal adj noc-tur-nal: of the night
His *nocturnal* wanderings through the woods go undetected by his neighbors.

nomad n no-mad: wanderer
The *nomad* was seen in every state.

nominate v nom-i-nate: to designate
She will surely be *nominated* for the chairperson's position.

nonchalant adj non-cha-lant: unconcerned
We assumed you did not like the movie because of your *nonchalant* manner.

norm n norm: standard
The *norm* in our neighborhood is for everyone to display a flag on July fourth.

nostalgia n nos-tal-gia: homesickness
Her *nostalgia* for her family was strengthened after seeing their photographs.

notarize v no-ta-rize: certify
You must certify the sale of your house by having the papers *notarized*.

notorious adj no-to-ri-ous: well known
Jesse James was a *notorious* bandit out West.

nourish v nour-ish: to make grow
Nourish the flowers now so that they will bloom in the spring.

novel adj nov-el: new
No one thinks of such *novel* ideas as the professor.

novel n nov-el: a relatively long fictional prose narrative
After receiving praise for his poems, the writer started work on a *novel*.

novice n no-vice: beginner
Although she is a *novice*, she swims very well.

nuisance n nui-sance: annoyance
All that traffic noise is a *nuisance* while I am trying to study.

nullify v nul-li-fy: to make void, to cancel
They *nullified* their vacation plans after the travel rates went up again.

numbness n numb-ness: loss of feeling
That bandage was wrapped so tightly that it left a *numbness* in his arm.

numismatics n nu-mis-mat-ics: study of coins
Numismatics is an interesting and profitable hobby.

O

obdurate adj ob-du-rate: stubborn
They won't be able to settle anything if they both stay as *obdurate* as they've been.

obese adj o-bese: very fat
If you keep eating that way, you will soon be *obese*.

obituary n o-bit-u-ar-y: notice of death
The *obituary* in the newspaper announced the demise of the editor.

objective n ob-jec-tive: aim, goal
The painter's *objective* is to see his art on display in the museum.

oblige v o-blige: compel, force
She was *obliged* to attend the meeting.

oblique adj ob-lique: slanting
Don't place any heavy objects against the *oblique* side of that building.

obliterate v ob-lit-er-ate: to destroy, blot out
The tornado *obliterated* the downtown district.

obnoxious adj ob-nox-ious: disagreeable
Nobody wanted to be around the *obnoxious* man.

obscene adj ob-scene: indecent, impure
Such *obscene* language is not allowed here.

obscure adj ob-scure: not clear, dim
Your statements seem too *obscure* this early in the morning.

obscure v ob-scure: to conceal
The fog *obscured* our view of the gardens.

obsess v ob-sess: fill the mind, haunt
She is *obsessed* by constant thoughts of food.

obsolete adj ob-so-lete: no longer in use
He had difficulty finding parts for his *obsolete* lawnmower.

obstacle n ob-sta-cle: hindrance
Please remove that *obstacle* from our path so that we may continue on.

obstinate adj ob-sti-nate: stubborn
She refused to budge from her *obstinate* opinion.

obstreperous adj ob-strep-er-ous: noisy, boisterous
That class is particularly *obstreperous*.

obstruction n ob-struc-tion: obstacle
An *obstruction* in the plans will delay completion of the project.

obtuse adj ob-tuse: blunt, not sharp
He did not understand because of his *obtuse* wit.

occult adj oc-cult: mysterious, magical
His *occult* attitude made us suspicious.

ocular adj oc-u-lar: of the eye
Keep those tools away from the *ocular* region.

odious adj o-di-ous: very displeasing
An *odious* sound emitted from the cellar.

odor n o-dor: scent, smell
The *odor* of food cooking filled the building.

offal n of-fal: garbage, refuse
Place any *offal* in the containers around the corner.

offensive adj of-fen-sive: on the attack
His *offensive* behavior annoyed the guests.

offensive n of-fen-sive: attitude, position, or operation of attack
It was a famous military *offensive*.

ogre n o-gre: monster
The child was afraid an *ogre* would appear in her room in the night.
olfactory adj ol-fac-to-ry: of smell
An animal's *olfactory* senses are more developed than a human's.
ominous adj om-i-nous: bad omen
The sudden cold weather created an *ominous* sign of winter ahead.

omniscient adj om-nis-cient: all-knowing
His *omniscient* gaze made the children fear that he was aware of what they had done.
omnivorous adj om-niv-o-rous: eating both animal and vegetable matter
We are *omnivorous* animals.
onerous adj on-er-ous: burdensome
Everyone avoids those kinds of *onerous* tasks.
onset n on-set: attack
An *onset* of poison ivy covered his body after he fell in the bushes.
onus n o-nus: responsibility
The *onus* is on the caretaker to keep the land in good condition.

ooze v ooze: slow flow
Ketchup *oozed* out of the crack in the bottle.
opaque adj o-paque: not transparent
They painted the walls in a dark, *opaque* color.
opiate n o-pi-ate: narcotic
An *opiate* was given to the patient to dull his pain.
opponent n op-po-nent: adversary
The officer and his *opponent* argued their views.

oppress v op-press: govern harshly
He *oppressed* his nation with his rigid rules.
optical adj op-ti-cal: of the eyes, visual
His *optical* senses were strengthened when his hearing weakened.
optimal adj op-ti-mal: most favorable
They will decide which is the *optimal* course of action.
option n op-tion: choice
Their only *option* is to eat at a restaurant tonight.

opulent adj op-u-lent: wealthy
They lived in an *opulent* neighborhood.
oracle n or-a-cle: prophet, priest
People crowded round the *oracle* to hear his sermon.
oral adj o-ral: spoken
An *oral* review of your book will be heard tonight.
oration n o-ra-tion: long speech
The tired guests tried in vain to stay awake throughout the *oration*.

orb n orb: sphere, globe
They traveled around the *orb* of the planet.

ordain v or-dain: to order, appoint
The committee *ordained* him as secretary of the organization.

ordinance n or-di-nance: rule, decree
The *ordinance* forbids swimming in the fountain.

orgy n or-gy: wild, drunken revel
Many people celebrate the arrival of the new year in an *orgy* of partying.

oriel n o-ri-el: bay window
Their new house offers a lovely *oriel* overlooking the hill.

orifice n or-i-fice: mouth, opening
Close your *orifice* when in water.

origin n or-i-gin: source, root
The *origin* of their family goes back to England.

orthodox adj or-tho-dox: customary
It is *orthodox* to leave your keys at the front desk.

orthopedist n or-tho-pe-dist: bone doctor
If you think you broke your finger, have it checked by an *orthopedist*.

oscillate v os-cil-late: to vary, swing
Her singing *oscillated* up and down the scales.

osprey n os-prey: sea hawk
From the boat's deck, we took pictures of the *osprey*.

ostensibly adv os-ten-si-bly: apparently
They have *ostensibly* decided to go ahead with your plans.

ostentatious adj os-ten-ta-tious: showy, vulgar
She paraded by in her new coat in such an *ostentatious* manner that she offended many people.

ostracize v os-tra-cize: to banish
The leader of the tribe *ostracized* the offender.

outlandish adj out-land-ish: ridiculous
His suggestions were *outlandish*.

outpost n out-post: guard
Station an *outpost* at the entrance to the museum.

outrageous adj out-ra-geous: shocking
Such an *outrageous* display of bad manners will not be tolerated here.

outstrip v out-strip: pass, excel
Autos in the left lane *outstrip* those in the right lane.

oval adj o-val: egg-shaped
Don't you agree that an *oval* table would best suit this room?

overcast adj o-ver-cast: cloudy, gloomy
The skies are too *overcast* to get a sunburn today.

overseer n over-seer: supervisor, foreman
He was appointed *overseer* of the family trust.
overwhelm v over-whelm: overpower, crush
All this homework is *overwhelming* me.
overwhelm adj over-whelm: above normal size
His *overwhelming* size scared the tiny children.
ovum n o-vum: egg
They examined the *ovum* under the microscope.

P

pachyderm n pach-y-derm: elephant, hippo
The *pachyderm* at the zoo is the most popular attraction.
pacific adj pa-cif-ic: peaceful, calm
Only a slight breeze blew in from the *pacific* water.
packet n pack-et: small parcel
I'm sure that *packet* will fit into my bag.
pact n pact: agreement
They signed a *pact* to keep peace between their nations.
pageant n pag-eant: procession
The *pageant* started at one end of town and ended at the other.
pagoda n pa-go-da: tower, temple
My favorite place to lunch in the park is near the *pagoda* in the gardens.
palatable adj pal-at-a-ble: agreeable
I did not find his suggestion *palatable*, and I refused to go along with it.
palate n pal-ate: roof of the mouth
He made clicking noises with his tongue on his *palate*.
pallid adj pal-lid: pale, lacking color
That frightening experience left a *pallid* expression on their faces.
palomino n pal-o-mi-no: cream-colored horse
Her favorite animal on the farm is the *palomino*.
palpitate v pal-pi-tate: tremble
His heart began to *palpitate* in anticipation of her arrival.
paltry adj pal-try: almost worthless
We might as well have no meat than that *paltry* amount.

pamper v pam-per: to indulge too much
They *pamper* their baby by allowing him anything he wants.

panacea n pan-a-ce-a: remedy, cure all
The *panacea* for your cold is to get lots of sleep and drink lots of liquids.

panda n pan-da: black and white bear
One of the favorite attractions at the zoo is the *panda*.

pandemonium n pan-de-mo-ni-um: tumult
Pandemonium resulted when the snake escaped from the cage into the crowd.

pang n pang: sharp pain
All that running caused a *pang* in his side.

panorama n pan-o-ra-ma: wide view
The windows offered a *panorama* of the city.

paragon n par-a-gon: model of excellence
His grades serve as a *paragon* for the rest of the students.

paramount n par-a-mount: supreme
It is *paramount* that this report be finished today.

paranoia n par-a-noi-a: mental disorder, fear of persecution
She is hoping that the therapy will cure her *paranoia*.

paraphernalia n par-a-pher-na-lia: equipment
Be sure to lock up all your *paraphernalia* at the end of each day.

parasite n par-a-site: hanger on
Too many *parasites* clustered around the actor's door.

parcel n par-cel: package
Please send that *parcel* to him in time for the holidays.

parcel v par-cel: to divide into portions
So many people wanted to taste the pie that I had to *parcel* it into many pieces.

parch v parch: dry by roasting
She *parched* the meat in the oven.

pare v pare: to cut, shave
Pare the potatoes into medium-size pieces.

pariah n pa-ri-ah: outcast
He was considered a *pariah* from the rest of that group.

parka n par-ka: jacket
Better wear your *parka* and boots when you go out in that blizzard.

parody n par-o-dy: imitation
The actress presented a brilliant *parody* of the character.

parole n pa-role: release of a prisoner before sentence expires
His *parole* from jail came unexpectedly.

parole v pa-role: to release on parole
Because of overcrowded cells, guards *paroled* several prisoners.

parry v par-ry: evade
I need your answer, so don't *parry* the question.

parsimonious adj par-si-mo-ni-ous: stingy
She is so *parsimonious* that she doesn't leave tips.

partisan n par-ti-san: supporter
His successful campaigning is bringing many *partisans* over to his side.

partition n par-ti-tion: division
Place the *partition* here so that we may have two rooms instead of one.

pastel adj pas-tel: pale shade of a color
Redo the bedroom in *pastel* colors.

pastel n pas-tel: a crayon of ground coloring
Use the *pastel* on this sheet.

paternal adj pa-ter-nal: fatherly
He treated the boys on his team with a *paternal* attitude.

pathetic adj pa-thet-ic: pitiful
It was such a *pathetic* sight that she burst into tears.

patience n pa-tience: tolerance
Try to keep your *patience* around the crowds.

patron n pa-tron: supporter
The performing arts organizations seek *patrons* to back their productions.

pattern n pat-tern: arrangement
The *pattern* created by the fallen leaves was interesting.

paucity n pau-ci-ty: scarcity; lack
A *paucity* of food is creating a panic in the camp.

paunch n paunch: stomach
Tuck your shirt in so that it covers your *paunch*.

pauper n pau-per: very poor person
The *pauper* continued to wear the same ragged coat every day.

peal v peal: loud, long sound
The church bells *pealed* from the loft.

peal n peal: the loud ringing of a bell or bells
The *peal* filled the village with pleasant sounds.

peasant n peas-ant: farmer
The *peasants* harvested their fall crops together.

peculiar adj pe-cul-iar: strange, odd
It seems so *peculiar* to walk barefoot after wearing shoes all year.

pedagogue n ped-a-gogue: teacher
Listen to the lessons of the *pedagogue*.

peddle v ped-dle: travel about and sell
They *peddled* their ceramics during the summer months.

pedestrian n pe-des-tri-an: walker
The *pedestrians* waited on the corner for the light to change.

pedigree n ped-i-gree: ancestry
Her *pedigree* dates back to the first settlers in this country.

peerless adj peer-less: matchless
They are the first-place team because their team members are *peerless*.

peevish adj pee-vish: irritable
He was very *peevish* when he found out he had failed the test.

penance n pen-ance: punishment
His *penance* for behaving badly was to go without supper.

penitentiary n pen-i-ten-tia-ry: prison
Criminals are locked up in the *penitentiary* until their sentence is over.

pensive adj pen-sive: thoughtful
Her *pensive* treatment of her guests met with sighs of approval.

penurious adj pe-nu-ri-ous: stingy
Although he is extremely rich, he is quite *penurious* with his money.

perch v perch: to roost, sit high
The pigeons *perched* on the telephone wire.

perch n perch: a horizontal pole; small spiny-finned fish
That telephone pole serves as a popular *perch* for birds.
The boy caught three *perch*.

perdition n per-di-tion: utter loss; hell
The town's *perdition* was caused by the flood.
The man's soul was bound for *perdition*.

perennial adj per-en-ni-al: unceasing
His *perennial* playing is getting on her nerves.

perfunctory adj per-func-to-ry: done mechanically
She was so tired, she typed in a *perfunctory* manner.

perigree n per-i-gee: closest point in orbit
The rocket was visible as it approached its *perigee*.

peril n per-il: danger
The *peril* in entering the wilderness alone is that there is no one to protect you.

peril v per-il: to expose to harm or injury
He *periled* himself by climbing the mountain.

perimeter n pe-rim-e-ter: boundary
They erected a fence around the *perimeter* of their land.

perish v per-ish: to be destroyed
The man *perished* in the earthquake.

perjure v per-jure: to swear falsely
He *perjured* himself by blaming his friends.

perpendicular adj per-pen-dic-u-lar: at right angles
The *perpendicular* arrangement was pleasing to the eye.

perpendicular n per-pen-dic-u-lar: a line at right angles to another line
A *perpendicular* is formed in the corner.

perpetrate v per-pe-trate: to commit, do
The crime was *perpetrated* by that person against the wall.

perpetual adj per-pet-u-al: eternal
The cemetery is responsible for the *perpetual* care of the gravesite.

perplex v per-plex: puzzle, confuse
The footsteps outside her door *perplexed* her.

persecute v per-se-cute: treat badly
He *persecuted* his younger sister until his parents made him stop.

persevere v per-se-vere: to persist
You will have to *persevere* with your project if you wish to be finished tonight.

persist v per-sist: to continue
Please *persist* with what you were doing until your turn arrives.

perspiration n per-spi-ra-tion: sweat
The *perspiration* shook off his body as he ran on.

pert adj pert: jaunty, lively, vivacious
The *pert* young lady became a cheerleader.

perturb v per-turb: disturb
Try to be quiet so that you don't *perturb* the readers.

peruse v pe-ruse: read thoroughly
Peruse the map before you attempt to drive this road.

pessimism n pes-si-mism: gloomy outlook
He always faces Monday mornings with *pessimism*.

pester v pes-ter: to annoy
The dog is *pestering* his owner for dinner.

pestilence n pes-ti-lence: disease, epidemic
A *pestilence* struck down the vacationers.

petrify v pet-ri-fy: turn to stone
The ancient bones *petrified* over a period of several hundred years.

petty adj pet-ty: small
Such a *petty* amount of money will not buy much.

philander v phi-lan-der: to flirt
The coy young girl *philandered* with the boys.

philanthropy n phi-lan-thro-py: love of mankind
He was recognized for his *philanthropy*.

philharmonic adj phil-har-mon-ic: organization of music
A beautiful *philharmonic* sound filled the church.

philharmonic n phil-har-mon-ic: a society that sponsors a symphony orchestra
The *philharmonic* will present two concerts this weekend.

phobic adj pho-bic: morbidly fearful
Ever since her near drowning as a child, she is *phobic* about swimming.

phonetics n pho-net-ics: science of sound
Phonetics is his specialty.

phrenetic adj phre-net-ic: frenzied, fanatic
The dogs ran around the house at a *phrenetic* pace.

pier n pier: dock, wharf
They always sit at the end of the *pier* to fish.

pigment n pig-ment: coloring matter
Use more *pigment* in that picture to make it more noticeable.

pilfer v pil-fer: to steal
He was so hungry that he *pilfered* eggs from the farmer's hen house.

pilgrim n pil-grim: wanderer
Pilgrims landed on the coast and set out to find the nearest village.

pillage v pil-lage: to rob, plunder
Pirates *pillaged* the ship after overtaking it.

pillage n pil-lage: loot
When the police broke in to the house, they discovered the stolen *pillage*.

pinnacle n pin-na-cle: highest point
His goal is to climb to the *pinnacle* of that mountain.

pious adj pi-ous: devout, religious
She spoke about her experiences in a *pious* manner.

piquant adj pi-quant: stimulating
Her *piquant* performance brought the audience to their feet in enthusiastic applause.

pitch n pitch: tar
The maintenance crew poured fresh *pitch* onto the road.

pitch v pitch: to throw
He *pitched* the ball over the wall.

pitch n pitch: act or manner of pitching
Her *pitch* was too high.

pithy adj pith-y: substantial, significant
Her *pithy* comments were always appreciated by her students.

pittance n pit-tance: small amount
Although your fee is only a *pittance*, it is sufficient to pay the bills.

placate v pla-cate: to soothe, satisfy
Such sweet music should *placate* his foul mood.

placid adj pla-cid: calm, quiet
A *placid* breeze greeted them when they opened the door.

plagiarize v pla-gia-rize: to copy from another
He was accused of *plagiarizing* his term paper.

plague n plague: disease, epidemic
An undefined *plague* struck the town, leaving all the residents ill.

plague v plague: to afflict with a plague; to vex, torment
A swarm of mosquitos *plagued* the campers.
His gout *plagued* him every time it rained.

plaintive adj plain-tive: sad; mournful
Plaintive cries were heard at the funeral.

plaudit n plau-dit: praise
The *plaudits* he heard from his fans were well-deserved.

plausible adj plau-si-ble: reasonable
Your conclusions are *plausible* to us.

plea n plea: request, appeal
Her *plea* was granted by the king.

pliable adj pli-a-ble: easily bent, flexible
He used *pliable* wire to get into the sewer grating.

plod v plod: walk heavily, trudge
The vendor *plodded* on, loaded down by his merchandise.

plume n plume: large feather
Her hat featured a purple *plume.*

plume v plume: to adorn with plumes
Plume the costume at the last moment.

plunder v plun-der: rob
Criminals *plundered* the warehouse for merchandise.

plunder n plun-der: something taken by force or theft
They were discovered hiding out with the *plunder* from the warehouse robbery.

poach v poach: trespass
He fenced in his land so that hunters would not *poach* on it.

poach v poach: to cook
Poach the eggs on the stove's back burner.

podiatrist n po-di-a-trist: foot doctor
You'd better have a *podiatrist* examine your toe injury.

podium n po-di-um: platform
The spotlight shone on the *podium.*

poise n poise: composure, balance
Her *poise* was upset when the kids ran through the house.

pollute v pol-lute: to make dirty, defile
Those gas fumes will *pollute* the air.

pompous adj pom-pous: acting proudly
The *pompous* professor strutted around his classroom.
ponder v pon-der: to consider
They *pondered* which way to turn at the fork in the road.
porous adj po-rous: full of tiny holes
This *porous* boat will not float.
porridge n por-ridge: oatmeal, mush
The *porridge* was getting cold.
portent n por-tent: warning; omen
The ringing of the alarm bell sounded a *portent* of invaders.
portfolio n port-fo-li-o: briefcase
His *portfolio* presented a report of the company's activities in the past year.
portly adj port-ly: stout, corpulent
She will never be able to stuff her *portly* figure into that tiny outfit.
portray v por-tray: to describe
He *portrayed* the woman he met at the party in his novel.
possess v pos-sess: to control, own
He wanted to *possess* the complete set of books.
Germany *possessed* France and Poland during World War II.
postdate v post-date: future date
Postdate that letter for next week.
posterior adj pos-te-ri-or: back, rear
The *posterior* view of the house is more appealing than the front.
posterior n pos-te-ri-or: the buttocks
She could not sit on her *posterior* for a while after receiving the shot.
posthumous adj post-hu-mous: after death
His widow received the *posthumous* prize.
posture n pos-ture: position of the body
Your *posture* will improve if you don't slouch in that chair.
potable adj po-ta-ble: fit for drinking
Keep that milk in the refrigerator so that it will be *potable* tomorrow.
potable n po-ta-ble: something drinkable
Potables will be available after the meal.
potent adj po-tent: powerful
A *potent* fuel in the engine caused the diesel to travel faster.
potion n po-tion: drink
The hostess prepared a special *potion* for her guest of honor.
poultry n poul-try: fowl, chickens
That market offers a wide selection of *poultry*.
prank n prank: playful trick
He is continually pulling *pranks* on his brothers.

prattle v prat-tle: foolish talk
Don't *prattle* on while I am trying to read.

preamble n pre-am-ble: introduction, preface
The *preamble* to the book was very informative.

precede v pre-cede: go before
A short introduction *preceded* his dance.

precept n pre-cept: rule of action
Follow the *precepts* that the law states.

precinct n pre-cinct: district
Each salesperson was assigned to a different *precinct*.

precious adj pre-cious: valuable
I suggest you store your *precious* jewelry in a safe place.

precipice n pre-ci-pice: steep cliff
They tried, but it was impossible to climb the *precipice*.

precise adj pre-cise: exact, accurate
We need a *precise* count of the number of people who attend.

preclude v pre-clude: prevent
You can *preclude* accidents by being careful.

prejudice n prej-u-dice: unfair opinion, bias
His *prejudice* interfered with his judgement.

prejudice v prej-u-dice: to injure or harm
She *prejudiced* her chances of getting elected by making that statement.

premonition n pre-mo-ni-tion: forewarning
She had a *premonition* that it would snow today.

prerogative n pre-rog-a-tive: right, privilege
It is his *prerogative* to spend his allowance as he wishes.

presage n pre-sage: omen
In a *presage* of success, they celebrated.

preserve v pre-serve: to save
They tried to *preserve* the whale that had washed up on shore.

preserve n pre-serve: place where game are maintained
They took their children to the *preserve* to see the animals.

presume v pre-sume: suppose
Don't *presume* you know everything about the incident.

pretext n pre-text: excuse, pretense
His *pretext* for staying home was that he was sick.

prevail v pre-vail: to win
You'll be in first place if you *prevail* in the race.

prevaricate v pre-var-i-cate: lie
When one is sworn in on the witness stand, he is not allowed to *prevaricate*.

prim adj prim: proper, formal
He insists that his children are *prim* and proper.
primitive adj prim-i-tive: simple
We prefer *primitive* ideas to complicated ones.
primitive n prim-i-tive: a primitive person or thing
He is the last *primitive* alive from that tribe.
principal adj prin-ci-pal: main, chief
The *principal* reason for this meeting is to select a new chairperson.
principal n prin-ci-pal: a governing officer, as of a school
Every Friday afternoon, the *principal* meets with all of the teachers.
principle n prin-ci-ple: ideal, belief
It is her *principle* that anyone can learn to play the piano.
prior adj pri-or: earlier, before
His *prior* speech was more didactic than this one.
probe v probe: investigate, search
The inspector *probed* the apartment for signs of the struggle.
probe n probe: a surgical instrument for exploring a wound
Doctors applied a *probe* to the man's chest to inspect the damage.
proboscis n pro-bos-cis: long snout
The *proboscis* on an anteater is particularly lengthy.
procure v pro-cure: obtain
She *procured* the letter from her uncle.
prodigal adj prod-i-gal: wasteful
The *prodigal* youth returned from his trip broke and tired.
prodigal n prod-i-gal: spendthrift
You're too much of a *prodigal* with your allowance.
prodigious adj pro-di-gious: great, huge
The *prodigious* size of the building prevented them from seeing around it.
prodigy n prod-i-gy: marvel, a wonder
He is considered to be a *prodigy* with computers.
profanity n pro-fan-i-ty: swearing
Refrain from using *profanity* around other people.
proficient adj pro-fi-cient: skilled, advanced
She is such a *proficient* typist that everyone prefers to hire her.
profound adj pro-found: deeply felt
The *profound* message of the play was successfully conveyed to the audience.
profuse adj pro-fuse: abundant, lavish
A *profuse* spread of food covered the table.
progeny n prog-e-ny: children, offspring
Their *progeny* are away at school most of the year.

prognosis n prog-no-sis: forecast
The weatherman's *prognosis* is for rain tomorrow.
prohibit v pro-hib-it: forbid, prevent
His father *prohibited* him from riding his bicycle in the park.
prolong v pro-long: to extend
This book is so good, I wish I could *prolong* the action.
prominent adj prom-i-nent: well known
Many fans came to see the *prominent* dancer perform.
promote v pro-mote: to raise, advance
She was *promoted* to the first ranks.
propel v pro-pel: to drive forward
An internal combustion engine *propels* the truck.
prosperous adj pros-per-ous: successful
His careful investments made him *prosperous*.
prostrate v pros-trate: lay down flat
He was *prostrate* under the car repairing the muffler.
prostrate adj pros-trate: lying face downward
She could not recognize him in that *prostrate* position.
protoplasm n pro-to-plasm: matter
Scientists are questioning that strange *protoplasm* found in his body.
provoke v pro-voke: to make angry, vex
She *provoked* him with her constant chatter.
proximity n prox-im-i-ty: nearness
The mouse quivered in fear from the *proximity* of the cat.
proxy n prox-y: agent, substitute
A *proxy* for the company presented their case.
prudent adj pru-dent: wise, sensible
Her *prudent* decision solved the problem.
pseudo adj pseu-do: false, sham
He was a *pseudo*-artist and merely played at painting.
puerile adj pu-er-ile: childish
His *puerile* actions surprised his co-workers.
pugilist n pu-gi-list: boxer, fighter
A boxing match will be held today to determine the best *pugilist* here.
pulsate v pul-sate: throb, vibrate
Her head began to *pulsate* from the effects of the medicine.
puma n pu-ma: wildcat
Several residents in the country reported seeing a *puma* in the hills.
pummeling n pum-mel-ing: beat with a fist
He received such a *pummeling* from that gang that he was hospitalized.

pummel v pum-mel: to beat with a fist
  She *pummeled* the wall when she heard the bad news.
punctual adj punc-tu-al: prompt
  The show starts exactly at eight, so please be *punctual*.
pungent adj pun-gent: stinging, sharp
  The ointment left a *pungent* sensation on his skin.
puny adj pu-ny: weak
  The abandoned kittens were *puny* from lack of care.
purge v purge: to cleanse
  Purge your mind of such wicked thoughts.
purge n purge: act of cleaning out
  Administrators felt a *purge* was in order.
pursue v pur-sue: chase, follow
  He would not *pursue* her any longer.
purvey v pur-vey: to supply, provide
  The neighbors *purveyed* food and clothing for the new tenants.
pusillanimous adj pu-sil-lan-i-mous: cowardly
  His *pusillanimous* actions did not scare off his attackers.
putrid adj pu-trid: rotten, foul
  A *putrid* odor escaped from the basement.
pygmy n pyg-my: dwarf
  The *pygmy* made up for his lack of size with his might.
python n py-thon: snake (boa)
  She was relieved to see that the *python* was kept in a sealed cage.

Q

quack n quack: false doctor, pretender
  Victims of the *quack* voiced their indignations to the authorities.
quack v quack: to utter the cry of a duck
  Ducks *quacked* as they paddled around the pond.
quack adj quack: fraudulent
  A *quack* certificate was discovered in the papers.
quadruped n quad-ru-ped: a fourfooted animal, having four feet
  These tracks indicate they were made by a *quadruped*.
quagmire n quag-mire: soft, muddy ground
  The pigs rolled around in the *quagmire*.
quaint adj quaint: amusing, pleasing
  What a *quaint* little dog that is.

quake v quake: shake, tremble
The poundings of the construction crew caused the ground to *quake*.

qualified v qual-i-fied: competent
If they consider you *qualified*, chances are good that you will get the job.

qualms n qualms: doubts
I have *qualms* about understanding all that is written here.

quantity n quan-ti-ty: amount
Tell the clerk the *quantity* you will need so that he can have adequate supplies available.

quarantine n quar-an-tine: period of detention and isolation
A *quarantine* was set up for those children with measles.

quarrel v quar-rel: dispute, fight
They *quarrelled* about who would use the car tonight.

quarrel n quar-rel: a cause for dispute
A *quarrel* erupted between the two shoppers when they both grabbed the same merchandise.

quarry n quar-ry: stone mine
Each year that *quarry* is dug deeper and deeper.

quartz n quartz: a hard mineral
While hiking up the mountain, they found several pieces of *quartz*.

quaver v qua-ver: to shake, tremble
The earthquake caused the ground to *quaver* for several minutes.

queasy adj quea-sy: easily upset
Her *queasy* stomach makes traveling unpleasant for her.

quench v quench: to put an end to
He *quenched* his thirst by drinking lots of water.

querulous adj quer-u-lous: complaining
Querulous residents told the building owner to make the repairs immediately.

query n que-ry: question
Her *query* had an obvious answer.

query v que-ry: to question
The police *queried* the suspect about the robbery.

quest n quest: hunt; search
A team of twenty men set out on the *quest*.

quill n quill: stiff feather
She found several *quills* by the duck pond

quip n quip: witty saying
He replied to her question with a *quip*.

quirk n quirk: peculiar way of acting
He is remembered for his *quirks*.

R

rabble n rab-ble: disorderly crowd
A *rabble* is gathering where the protestors are marching.

rabies n ra-bies: dog disease
The dog received his annual *rabies* shot.

radical adj rad-i-cal: extreme
Most voters do not support him because of his *radical* views.

rafter n raf-ter: slanting beam
The cabin's roof is supported by several *rafters*.

rage n rage: violent anger
His *rage* scared off anyone from approaching him.

rage v rage: to show violent anger
She *raged* at the motorist who backed into her car.

raid n raid: attack
The troops staged a *raid* on the enemy camp.

raid v raid: to make a raid on, to take part in a raid
She *raided* the storage closet for extra supplies.

rally v ral-ly: to bring together
Members of the family *rallied* for a reunion at the campsite.

rally n ral-ly: a gathering
They met after twenty years at a massive *rally*.

ramble v ram-ble: to wander about
On this pleasant day, several people *rambled* through the park.

rambunctious adj ram-bunc-tious: unruly, wild
Not many people can handle her *rambunctious* behavior.

rampage n ram-page: state of excitement or rage, wild behavior
The untamed dogs went on a *rampage* throughout the countryside.

rancid adj ranc-id: stale, spoiled
The meat became *rancid* after lying in the refrigerator for a week.

rancor n ran-cor: hatred
His *rancor* showed through his attempts to be civil to his neighbors.

random adj ran-dom: by chance
Take a *random* sample of the population to find out if your idea is good.

ransack v ran-sack: to search, rob
Somebody broke into their house and *ransacked* it.

rant v rant: speak wildly
He *ranted* about his episodes in the city.

rapier n ra-pier: sword
His costume was not complete until he added his *rapier*.

rapport n rap-port: harmony, agreement
An instant *rapport* developed between the new neighbors and the old tenants.

rarefy v rar-e-fy: purify, refine
She *rarefied* the room with a thorough cleaning.

rash adj rash: careless, hasty
It is better to take your time deciding than to make a *rash* answer.

rash n rash: an eruption on the body
When she had the measles, it showed up as a *rash* on her face and arms.

rasp v rasp: harsh, grating sound
A *rasp* escaped from her throat as she endured the fifth day of her cold.

rasp n rasp: a type of file
Hand me the *rasp* so that I can finish this job.

ratify v rat-i-fy: approved, confirm
Two-thirds of the population have to *ratify* the decision before it is considered accepted.

ration n ra-tion: fixed allowance
If you continue that *ration* of food daily, you will surely gain weight.

ration v ra-tion: to furnish with rations, to hand out
You will have to *ration* the remaining supplies carefully.

rational adj ra-tio-nal: sensible
Study the situation clearly so that you present a *rational* conclusion.

ravage v rav-age: to damage greatly
The tornado *ravaged* the land.

ravage n rav-age: ruin, destruction
The *ravage* brought on the town by the storm was beyond repair.

rave v rave: to talk wildly, to talk incoherently
In his excitement, he *raved* about the accident he witnessed.

rave n rave: a very enthusiastic commendation
She endorsed her candidate with a *rave*.

ravenous adj rav-e-nous: very hungry, greedy
I am *ravenous* for that steak.

ravishing adj rav-ish-ing: delightful
Your friend is a very *ravishing* man.

raze v raze: to tear down, destroy
The construction crew had to *raze* the old building before laying the foundation for the new one.

realm n realm: kingdom
The queen's *realm* consists of this entire continent.

reap v reap: to cut, gather
At the end of the summer season, farmers *reap* the crop.

rebate n re-bate: partial refund
When he cancelled his travel plans, the travel agency sent him a *rebate*.

rebate v re-bate: to give back part of payment
When you return the remainder of the machine, the office will-*rebate* the amount stated.

rebuke v re-buke: scold, reprove
He *rebuked* his daughter for running out into the street.

recalcitrant adj re-cal-ci-trant: disobedient
Some people send their *recalcitrant* dogs to schools to be trained.

recapitulate v re-ca-pit-u-late: repeat
Please *recapitulate* the instructions you gave this morning.

receptacle n re-cep-ta-cle: container
You will find a *receptacle* in the corner for your leftovers.

recipient n re-cip-i-ent: receiver
The *recipient* of the package was delighted.

reciprocal adj re-cip-ro-cal: in return
A *reciprocal* agreement will allow both sides to be satisfied.

reciprocal n re-cip-ro-cal: a complement, mathematical counterpart
The *reciprocal* of ½ is ⅔.

reckless adj reck-less: rash; careless
His *reckless* behavior will get him into trouble.

reckon v reck-on: to count, compute, to estimate
Reckon the figures and enter the result on the bill.

recline v re-cline: lean back
If your back is aching, *recline* against this pole.

recluse n re-cluse: hermit
He has become a *recluse* since his family moved away.

recoil v re-coil: to shrink back
She *recoiled* from the fire.

recoil n re-coil: a drawing away from
They were offended by his *recoil* from their pet.

recollect v rec-ol-lect: remember
Try to *recollect* everything that happened to you a year ago today.

recompense n re-com-pense: reward, pay back
His *recompense* for good behavior was a trip to the park.

recompense v re-com-pense: to repay or reward
They *recompensed* him for his generosity.

reconcile v re-con-cile: to settle
She *reconciled* their disagreement and they shook hands.

recuperate v re-cu-per-ate: to recover
She is still *recuperating* from the measles.

recurrence n re-cur-rence: repetition
This dream is a *recurrence* of the one I had a week ago.
redeem v re-deem: buy back
You can *redeem* your boat for the same price you sold it to me.
redundant adj re-dun-dant: not needed; extra
Your essay is filled with *redundant* statements.
reek n reek: unpleasant smell
A *reek* escaped from the trash can when the lid was lifted.
reek v reek: to emit a strong offensive smell
That spoiled food *reeks*.
referendum n ref-er-en-dum: voting
We will decide tomorrow at the *referendum* if that law should be reinstated.
reflexive adj re-flex-ive: non-voluntary action
His *reflexive* shout when he won the prize caused everyone to look at him in surprise.
refract v re-fract: to bend a ray of light
The window *refracted* the sunlight.
refuge n ref-uge: shelter, safety
It was raining so hard that we ran to the trees for *refuge*.
refurbish v re-fur-bish: polish again
Refurbish the floor again to ensure a fine finish.
regal adj re-gal: royal, kingly
His status requires that he act in a *regal* manner.
regale v re-gale: entertain
He always *regales* us with his witty remarks.
regatta n re-gat-ta: boat race
A *regatta* will be held on Lake Erie on Saturday.
regulate v reg-u-late: to control
Regulate the amount of candy that you give to the children.
regurgitate v re-gur-gi-tate: to throw up
Many types of animals *regurgitate* their food.
rehabilitate v re-ha-bil-i-tate: restore
They tried to *rehabilitate* the old house to its former, elegant style.
rehash v re-hash: deal with again
We have already *rehashed* that problem, so let's go on to another one.
rehash n re-hash: a reworking, a new form
The newspaper presented a *rehash* of what we heard on television last night.
rehearse v re-hearse: practice
The actors *rehearsed* the scene again.
reimburse v re-im-burse: to pay back

She *reimbursed* her parents for their loan to her during her school years.

reincarnation n re-in-car-na-tion: rebirth
I always look forward to the *reincarnation* of warm weather each spring.

reiterate v re-it-er-ate: to repeat
The speaker *reiterated* the same passage to assure comprehension by the crowd.

rejuvenate v re-ju-ve-nate: to make young again
A good diet and daily exercise will *rejuvenate* you.

relentless adj re-lent-less: unyielding
This *relentless* ache in my back is bothering me.

reliable adj re-li-a-ble: trustworthy
The bank requires that all its employees be *reliable*.

relic n rel-ic: survival from the past, item of interest because of age
They brought back several *relics* found on their archaeological expedition.

relinquish v re-lin-quish: to abandon, give up
She *relinquished* her right to the estate.

relish n re-lish: an appetizing condiment
The casserole was topped with a delicious *relish*.

relish v rel-ish: to take pleasure in
He *relished* playing with his young daughter.

remiss adj re-miss: careless
She was *remiss* in her treatment of the book.

remit v re-mit: to send money
Please *remit* the amount you owe on your bill immediately.

remnant n rem-nant: small part left
Please ask the waiter to wrap the *remnant* of this steak so that I can take it home.

remonstrance n re-mon-strance: protest
The parents' *remonstrance* against the teacher's treatment was overwhelming.

remorse n re-morse: regret, sorrow
It is with *remorse* that I decline your invitation.

remote adj re-mote: distant, far away
A *remote* rumbling could be heard from the other side of the forest.

remunerate v re-mu-ner-ate: pay
The finance department will *remunerate* you for your work.

renaissance n re-nais-sance: revival
A *renaissance* of the movie brought old fans and new ones.

rendezvous n   ren-dez-vous: meeting
   She wore her favorite dress for their *rendezvous*.

renegade n   ren-e-gade: deserter, traitor
   A *renegade* from the troops was reported in this area.

renounce v   re-nounce: give up
   Sadly, the dieter *renounced* all fattening foods.

renovate v   ren-o-vate: renew, restore
   They are attempting to *renovate* the antique car to its former glory.

repartee n   re-par-tee: witty reply
   You never fail to think up delightful *repartee* to whatever anyone says.

repeal v   re-peal: to withdraw, take back
   She reconsidered selling her car and *repealed* her offer.

repel v   re-pel: force back, to cause dislike
   I am *repelled* by that decaying odor.

repent v   re-pent: regret
   After playing a trick on his friend, he *repented* his behavior.

repine v   re-pine: to be discontented
   The child *repined* for days at the loss of his puppy.

replete adj   re-plete: filled
   The menu was *replete* with dozens of desserts.

replica n   rep-li-ca: copy, reproduction
   A *replica* of that masterpiece is for sale.

repose n   re-pose: rest, sleep
   Look how peaceful she looks in her *repose*.

repose v   re-pose: to lie at rest
   You may *repose* on this sofa.

repress v   re-press: to keep down
   Try to *repress* the little boy's excitement in this room.

reprieve n   re-prieve: temporary delay
   They requested a *reprieve* from the insurance company until they could make their monthly payment.

reproach v   re-proach: to blame
   She *reproached* him for the broken glass even though it was not his fault.

reprove v   re-prove: scold, blame
   The teacher *reproved* her students for their noisy actions.

repugnant adj   re-pug-nant: distasteful
   That meat left a *repugnant* taste in my mouth.

rescind v   re-scind: to repeal, cancel
   His orders were *rescinded* this morning, so you are free to continue your research.

reservoir n res-er-voir: storehouse
A *reservoir* of merchandise is available if they run out of goods in the shop.

residence n res-i-dence: home, abode
My *residence* is a large house in the country.

residue n res-i-due: remainder
The *residue* of the shipwreck was washed up on shore.

resilience n re-sil-i-ence: elasticity
If you are not sure of the size you wear, buy something that has enough *resilience*.

resolute adj res-o-lute: determined, firm
A *resolute* look came over her face as she struggled on.

respiration n res-pi-ra-tion: breathing
The old man's illness slowed his *respiration*.

response n re-sponse: answer
His *response* was not the usual reply we receive to our inquiry.

restive adj res-tive: restless, uneasy
The animals are becoming *restive* from the sounds of thunder.

restrain v re-strain: hold back
It is hard to *restrain* her fans from following her.

resume n re-sum-e: summary
He included a *resume* at the end of his letter.

resume v re-sume: to begin again, go on
They *resumed* the game where they left off last week.

resurgent adj re-sur-gent: rising again
The *resurgent* tide reaches as far as that buoy every day.

retaliate v re-tal-i-ate: to pay back a wrong
He *retaliated* by playing a trick on them.

retard v re-tard: to make slow, delay
The heavy load in his car *retarded* his travels.

reticent adj ret-i-cent: reserved, silent
We assumed she was shy because of her *reticent* behavior.

retinue n ret-i-nue: followers, attendants
The *retinue* proceeded along the church aisle behind the bride and groom.

retort n re-tort: quick, sharp answer
She replied with a *retort* to his question.

retract v re-tract: to take back
I wish I could *retract* the unfair statement I made to him.

retrogress v ret-ro-gress: move backward
Living conditions have *retrogressed* since the flood.

revenge v re-venge: do harm in return
I will *revenge* my friend's murder.

revenge n   re-venge: desire to take vengeance
He will surely seek *revenge* because of what you did to him.

revenue n   rev-e-nue: income
Be sure to record all your *revenue* from the past year on the budget sheet.

reverberate v   re-ver-ber-ate: to reflect, echo
The sound of thunder *reverberated* through the canyon.

reverence n   rev-er-ence: respect
They were taught to treat their elders with *reverence*.

reverie n   rev-er-ie: dreamy thoughts
She wastes too much time in *reverie* when she should be working.

revile v   re-vile: to abuse, malign
The child *reviled* his friend because he was envious.

revise v   re-vise: to change, amend
Each year, they *revise* the schedule.

revoke (v)   re-voke: to cancel
His pass was *revoked* because he failed inspection.

ribald adj   rib-ald: offensive, indecent
Her *ribald* behavior kept her off the team.

ridicule v   rid-i-cule: make fun of, mock
She ran home crying after the other children *ridiculed* her clothes.

ridicule n   rid-i-cule: the act of making one the object of laughter
Their *ridicule* of her made her ashamed of her actions.

riffraff n   riffraff: worthless people
They fenced in their property to keep *riffraff* off their land.

rift n   rift: an opening caused by splitting
Water is leaking out of the *rift* in the pool.

righteous adj   righ-teous: virtuous, blameless
The child adopted a *righteous* attitude about his low test mark.

rigid adj   rig-id: firm, stiff
Soldiers stand in a *rigid* position for inspection.

rigor n   rig-or: strictness
His *rigor* prevented them from enjoying the class.

rite n   rite: ceremony
Each June, there is a *rite* for all the graduates.

rivet v   riv-et: to fasten firmly
Rivet yourself to the seat before takeoff.

rivet n   riv-et: metal bolt
The plane has approximately eight hundred *rivets* in its body.

roam v   roam: wander
Close the pen so that the cows cannot *roam* around the field.

robust adj   ro-bust: strong, healthy

All that exercise and sensible dieting has transformed him into a *robust* figure of a man.

rodent n ro-dent: gnawing animal
He suggested that we clean the apartment before moving in so that it would be free of *rodents*.

roe n roe: fish eggs; small nimble European deer
Some restaurants serve *roe* as a gourmet specialty.
He shot the graceful, nimble *roe*.

rogue n rogue: rascal
He is such a *rogue*, but everyone likes him.

roster n ros-ter: list
He kept a *roster* of the names of all the attendees.

rote n rote: repetition by memory
The actor presented the speech by *rote*.

rubbish n rub-bish: trash, litter, debris
Following the party, there was plenty of *rubbish* to be cleaned up.

ruddy adj rud-dy: healthy red color
A *ruddy* complexion shone on her face following her exercising.

rudimentary adj ru-di-men-ta-ry: elementary
She needs to complete her *rudimentary* education before entering college.

rueful adj rue-ful: sorrowful, regretful
She approached the storeowner with the broken dish in hand and a *rueful* expression on her face.

ruffian n ruf-fi-an: cruel person
He is truly a *ruffian* to pick on those boys like that.

ruffle n ruf-fle: pleated, gathered folds in material
He smoothed out the *ruffle* in the bedspread.

ruffle v ruf-fle: to disturb the smoothness of
She *ruffled* the water when she dropped the oar in the lake.

rummage v rum-mage: to search
They were *rummaging* through the attic in search of the old photographs.

rumor n ru-mor: general talk not based on definite knowledge
The *rumor* going around the office is that she will be promoted soon.

rupture v rup-ture: to break
The balloon *ruptured* into several pieces when it struck the pin.

rupture n rup-ture: a breaking apart
The *rupture* in the tire made the car swerve off the road.

rural adj ru-ral: of the country
I prefer the tranquility of a *rural* environment to the noise of the city.

ruse n ruse: scheme, trick
They concocted an elaborate *ruse* to keep her out of the house until evening.
rustic adj rus-tic: countryish, rural
Their home reflects the *rustic* surroundings of the town.
rustic n rus-tic: a country person
Why don't you ask a *rustic* for directions to the forest?

S

saber n sa-ber: sword
He faced his enemies with a *saber*.
saccharine adj sac-cha-rine: cloyingly sweet
Although she did not like him, she was extremely *saccharine* in her manner.
saccharine n sac-cha-rine: synthetic sweetener
He used *saccharine* in his coffee instead of sugar.
sacrifice n sac-ri-fice: offering
They presented a *sacrifice* on the altar.
saga n sa-ga: story of heroic deeds
They loved the *sagas* that the old man told to them every time they visited him.
sagacious adj sa-ga-cious: shrewd, wise
His *sagacious* advice has helped us solve many dilemmas.
sage adj sage: wise
The elders of this tribe render all *sage* decisions.
sage n sage: a very wise man; seasoning
People travel from great distances to seek advice from the *sage*.
She added *sage* to the sauce.
salient adj sa-li-ent: prominent, striking
His *salient* figure elicits trust from the people.
saline adj sa-line: salty
There was a *saline* taste in the water.
salon n sa-lon: large room
Guests will be most comfortable in the *salon*.
salubrious adj sa-lu-bri-ous: healthy
Part of her good mood is due to her *salubrious* state of mind and body.

salvage v sal-vage: to rescue
They *salvaged* all the remaining intact furniture from the ruins.

salvage n sal-vage: a rescued ship, crew, and cargo
They pulled the *salvage* of the boat onto shore.

salvation n sal-va-tion: saving
The minister tried to bring about a *salvation* of the gang.

salve n salve: ointment
Apply a *salve* to that wound right away.

salve v salve: to apply salve to
Salve the infection with this medicine.

sanatorium n san-a-to-ri-um: health resort
Following her long illness, she went off to a *sanatorium* to recover her strength.

sanctify v sanc-ti-fy: to make holy
His baptism was *sanctified* at the altar.

sanctuary n sanc-tu-ary: refuge, safe place
They ran to the barn for *sanctuary* from the strong wind.

sane adj sane: rational
We would prefer that you took your time and presented us with a *sane* decision.

sanguine adj san-guine: cheerful and hopeful
A *sanguine* expression appeared on his face as he saw his mother go to the candy dish.

sanitary adj san-i-tar-y: free from filth
You must keep the patients in *sanitary* conditions.

sapience n sa-pi-ence: wisdom
We value his words of *sapience*, based on his years of experience in that field.

sapling n sap-ling: young tree
They planted a *sapling* in the front yard in hopes that it would sprout leaves in the spring.

sardonic adj sar-don-ic: scornful
A *sardonic* expression appeared on her face when she saw him talking to the new girl in class.

satchel n satch-el: handbag
She always takes her *satchel* whenever she goes out.

satellite n sat-el-lite: orbiting sphere
The *satellite* beamed valuable information down to earth.

satiate v sa-ti-ate: satisfy fully
She *satiated* her hunger only when she had consumed the entire casserole.

satirize v sat-i-rize: to criticize, ridicule
She *satirized* his attempts to learn to ride the bike.

saturate v sat-u-rate: to soak thoroughly
Saturate the material with the dye if you want an even color.
saturnalia n sat-ur-na-li-a: wild merrymaking
Their victory was followed by a *saturnalia*, in which some damage was done to their house.
saucy adj sau-cy: rude
He answered her inquiry in a *saucy* tone.
savage adj sav-age: wild, rugged
This barren land is considered *savage* country.

savage n sav-age: member of a primitive human society
Savages protected their tribe from intruders.
savannah n sa-van-nah: treeless plain
Miles and miles of *savannah* spread out before them.
savor n sa-vor: taste or smell, flavor
The *savor* of meat made her hungry.
savor v sa-vor: to enjoy the characteristic taste, smell
He *savored* the smell of roast beef.
scaffold n scaf-fold: platform, stage
The artist stood on a *scaffold* to paint the mural on the wall.

scalawag n scal-a-wag: rascal, scamp
Her pet dog is such a lovable *scalawag*.
scald v scald: to burn
The oven *scalded* her hand when she got too close to the flame.
scald n scald: a burn caused by scalding
She applied ointment to the *scald* on her hand.
scallion n scal-lion: type of onion
He added some *scallions* to the stew for the final touch.

scallop n scal-lop: kind of shellfish, mollusk
For dinner tonight they will be serving *scallops* with vegetables.
scamper v scam-per: run quickly
After breaking the window, the boys *scampered* away out of sight.
scan v scan: to look closely, examine
She *scanned* the papers for errors.
scandal n scan-dal: shameful action
Their fight had created a *scandal* in the town.

scant adj scant: not enough
There won't be any extra desserts tonight since we only have a *scant* supply.
scarce adj scarce: rare, hard to get
Those types of pictures are very *scarce* and, thus, are valuable.
scarlet adj scar-let: bright red
We could spot her several blocks away in that *scarlet* jacket.

scathing adj scath-ing: severe
She gave him a *scathing* look when he questioned her.
scent n scent: smell
Her perfume left a pleasant *scent* in the room long after she had left.
scheme v scheme: to plan, plot
They *schemed* to give him a surprise party.
scheme n scheme: a systematic plan for obtaining some object
They established a *scheme* to put them in first place.
schism n schism: a split, break-up
After the *schism*, each partner started a new business.
schooner n schoon-er: sailing vessel
They traveled to Europe in a *schooner*.
sciatica n sci-at-i-ca: painful condition of the hip
His pain was diagnosed as *sciatica*.
scintilla n scin-til-la: very small amount
There was not one *scintilla* of food left in the closet.
scintillate v scin-til-late: to sparkle, flash
The diamonds *scintillated* in the bright light.
scoff v scoff: to make fun of, mock
They *scoffed* at his attempts to repair the engine.
scoff n scoff: a mock or jeer
Even though he failed in his efforts, he did not deserve the *scoff* he received from his friends.
scorch v scorch: to burn
He *scorched* his hand when he picked up the hot dish without a protecting mitt.
scorn n scorn: despise
His *scorn* was not easily disguised.
scour v scour: to clean; search thoroughly
She *scoured* the closet for her old dress. They *scoured* the attic.
scourge v scourge: to punish
The warden *scourged* the prisoners for their crimes.
scow n scow: flat boat
They glided across the lake in a *scow*.
scrawl n scrawl: careless handwriting
His *scrawl* is indecipherable.
scrawl v scrawl: to write or draw hastily
She *scrawled* the message on the first piece of paper she found so that she wouldn't forget it.
scrawny adj scraw-ny: skinny
Lack of food reduced him to a *scrawny* figure of a man.
scribe n scribe: writer
The *scribe* took down every word spoken at the meeting.

scrimp v scrimp: use sparingly
Until payday, we'll have to *scrimp* on groceries.

scruff n scruff: back of the neck
Be sure to wash the *scruff* of your neck.

scruple n scru-ple: inability to act because of conscience
His *scruples* would not let him support the candidate.

scrutinize v scru-ti-nize: to inspect, examine
She carefully *scrutinized* his homework for errors, but found none.

scurry v scur-ry: to run quickly, hurry
The field mouse *scurried* away from the cat.

scurry n scur-ry: a scampering
The *scurry* of little feet was heard in the nursery.

secede v se-cede: to withdraw
The South wanted to *secede* from the Union.

sect n sect: group, organization
A *sect* from the school meets here each Monday night to discuss
upcoming events.

secular adj sec-u-lar: worldly, not religious
He is noted for his *secular* views about mankind.

secure adj se-cure: safe, protected
A *secure* shed was constructed to protect their equipment.

sedate adj se-date: calm, quiet down
They met a *sedate* group of businessmen.

seduce v se-duce: to lead astray, beguile
He *seduced* the puppy away from her mother.

sedulous adj sed-u-lous: hard working
He completed the job in his customary *sedulous* manner.

seek v seek: to look for
He'll probably find his papers if he *seeks* in the desk.

seep v seep: to ooze, leak slowly
Water *seeped* from the bottom of the plant onto the carpet.

seethe v seethe: to be disturbed
The man *seethed* over his lost briefcase.

segment n seg-ment: part, section
A *segment* of this book will cover the events of the party.

segment v seg-ment: to divide into segments
He *segmented* the audience into two groups.

segregate v seg-re-gate: to set apart, separate
The slow-learning children were *segregated* from the rest of their
classmates.

seismology n seis-mol-o-gy: earthquake study
He understood the danger because of his knowledge of *seismology*.

seize v seize: to clutch, grab
She *seized* the nearest branch as she fell from the tree.

semantic n se-man-tic: pertaining to meaning of words
A study of English *semantics* will indicate similarities with other languages.

semblance n sem-blance: outward appearance
He displayed a *semblance* of calm although he was actually quite frightened.

sentiment n sen-ti-ment: tender feeling
His *sentiment* for his child is touching.

sentinel n sen-ti-nel: guard, sentry
Post a *sentinel* at the front and back doors during the display of the valuable collection.

sepia n se-pi-a: dark brown
Use *sepia* to dye your sofa that color.

sepia adj se-pi-a: dark brown
I suggest you use that *sepia* shade for your curtains.

sepulcher n sep-ul-cher: tomb, grave
Following her funeral, she was buried in the family *sepulcher*.

sequel n se-quel: continuation
A *sequel* to the book will be published soon.

sequence n se-quence: order of succession
Be sure to read the manuals in the proper *sequence*.

sequester v se-ques-ter: to remove
Officials *sequestered* the prisoner from the courtroom.

sequoia n se-quoi-a: tall tree
The *sequoia* blocked their view of the mountain range.

serene adj se-rene: calm, peaceful
A *serene* expression came over his face when he realized that everything was all right.

serf n serf: slave
The landowner treated his *serf* as if he was one of the family.

serpent n ser-pent: snake
She screamed when she saw the *serpent* in the garden.

sever v sev-er: to cut, break off, divide
The knife quickly *severed* the fruit into tiny pieces.

severe adj se-vere: strict, stern, harsh
He is following a *severe* diet and exercise plan to lose twenty pounds in time for the holidays.

shaft n shaft: spear, pole
They left for the hunt with *shafts* at their side.

shaft v shaft: to fit with a shaft
They *shafted* the roof to support it against the wind.

shallow adj shal-low: not deep
She let the kids wade in the *shallow* pool.
shallow n shal-low: a shoal
Signs were posted to keep boats out of the *shallow*.
sham n sham: pretense, fraud
His injury was an absolute *sham*.
sham adj sham: not real, false
He gave a *sham* portrayal of the character's actions.
sham v sham: to pretend, feign
He *shammed* an illness to get out of taking the exam.
shanty n shan-ty: cabin, hut
He lives in poverty in a *shanty* near the dump.
shatter v shat-ter: to break into pieces
The glass *shattered* all over the kitchen when she dropped it.
sheath n sheath: case for a knife
Store the knife in its *sheath* after each use so that it will stay in good
condition.
sheen n sheen: brightness, luster
He polished the fire engine to such a *sheen* that it looked new.
sheer adj sheer: very thin
A *sheer* layer of snow covered the valley.
sheer adv sheer: completely, utterly
A *sheer*, piercing shriek emitted from the machine.
sheik n sheik: Arab chief or leader
The *sheik* invited the foreign dignitaries into his quarters.
shiftless adj shift-less: lazy
He was fired from his job because of his *shiftless* activities.
shirk v shirk: to avoid work
He was fired because he *shirked* his job too often.
shirk n shirk: one who shirks
He probably won't get the job because of his reputation as a *shirk*.
shiver v shiv-er: to shake
The cold air made her *shiver* in her light clothes.
shoddy adj shod-dy: inferior
Their incompetent paint job gave the house a *shoddy* appearance.
shred n shred: fragment
A *shred* of glass remained on the floor.
shred v shred: to tear or cut into shreds
Shred this paper into small pieces.
shrewd adj shrewd: clever, astute
He was *shrewd* in the way he handled the situation.
shrill adj shrill: piercing sound
A *shrill* alarm went off when they tried to break into the house.

shrill v shrill: to make a high-pitched sound
Alarm bells *shrilled* as the intruders ran away.
shrivel v shriv-el: to dry up, to shrink
The flowers and plants began to *shrivel* during the drought.
shrub n shrub: bush
She hid in the *shrub* from her friends.

shudder v shud-der: to tremble
They *shuddered* in their light sweaters when the weather suddenly
turned cold.
shun v shun: to avoid
He *shuns* anyone who wants his advice.
shy adj shy: bashful
Her *shy* child did not say a word to the adults.
shy v shy: to move suddenly as if startled
Watch the passengers *shy* away when you place that grotesque object
on the seat.
siege n siege: attack
A *siege* started when the enemy troops encountered each other.
siesta n si-es-ta: nap, rest
If you are planning to be out late tonight, take a *siesta* this afternoon.
sieve n sieve: strainer
Remove all the water from the pasta by draining it in the *sieve*.
sift v sift: to separate
Sift the pebbles out of the sand.
significant adj sig-nif-i-cant: important
You will find a *significant* clue in this book.

silhouette n sil-hou-ette: outlined portrait
He had the artist draw a *silhouette* of his daughter to give to his wife
for her birthday.
silhouette v sil-hou-ette: to show against a bright background
He was *silhouetted* behind the flimsy curtain.
simian adj sim-i-an: apelike
He can climb trees with *simian* agility.

simmer v sim-mer: to boil gently
When the eggs have boiled, let them *simmer* for a while.
simpleton n sim-ple-ton: silly person
She is such a *simpleton* that no one takes her seriously.
simulate v sim-u-late: to feign, pretend
He *simulated* the actions of a lame person so that he could be ex-
cused from doing the exercises.
sincere adj sin-cere: honest, genuine
They trust her because of her *sincere* attitude.

sinecure n si-ne-cure: job requiring little work
If you are looking for a *sinecure* here, you've come to the wrong place.

singe n singe: slight burn
A *singe* appeared on the blouse where the iron had stayed too long.

singe v singe: to burn superficially or slightly
She *singed* her neck when the curling iron came too close to her skin.

sinister adj sin-is-ter: evil, threatening
He faced them at the door of his house with a *sinister* expression on his face.

sinuous adj sin-u-ous: with many curves
The *sinuous* road was hazardous at night.

sire n sire: male ancestor
Her *sire* left the house and property to her.

sire v sire: to beget
They *sired* seven children.

skeptical adj skep-ti-cal: doubting
Their *skeptical* expressions lead me to believe that they don't approve of my ideas.

skew v skew: to twist, slant
Skew the bottle cap to the right first.

skew n skew: swerve
The *skew* of the wheels sent the truck racing off the road.

skillet n skil-let: frying pan
I have all the kitchen utensils I need except a *skillet* large enough to fry potatoes.

skim v skim: remove from the top
Be careful to *skim* the grease off the top of the soup before reheating it.

skimpy adj skimp-y: scanty, not enough
You'll need to wear more than that *skimpy* outfit in this cold weather.

skirmish n skir-mish: conflict, argument
The sale of the property created a *skirmish* between family members.

skittish adj skit-tish: easily frightened
Don't take that *skittish* child into the haunted house.

slack adj slack: loose, not firm; slow, sluggish
They usually start their jobs on Monday mornings in a *slack* manner.
The rope hung *slack* over the wall.

slander n slan-der: false harmful remark
Avoid *slander* when talking about them.

slander v slan-der: to make a damaging statement about
His remarks *slandered* their reputation.

slapdash adj slap-dash: hasty and careless
His *slapdash* cleansing of the warehouse hardly improved the mess at all.
slapdash n slap-dash: carelessness
Her *slapdash* left the room looking untidy.
slash v slash: to cut, gash
He *slashed* his toe while mowing the lawn.
slash n slash: a gash
An ugly *slash* appeared on her arm where the back door had hit her.
slay v slay: to kill with violence
Someone has been *slaying* the sheep.
sleazy adj sleaz-y: flimsy
That *sleazy* dress is not appropriate for such a formal affair.
sleek adj sleek: soft and glossy
The car has such a *sleek* surface.
sleet n sleet: frozen rain
Bundle up warmly and take an umbrella to protect you from the *sleet*.
sleet v sleet: to shower in the form of sleet
Instead of a blizzard, it *sleeted* all day.
sleuth n sleuth: detective
They hired a *sleuth* to uncover the reason for her actions.
slime n slime: mud, filth
She fell into the *slime* and ruined her dress.
slipshod adj slip-shod: careless, untidy
She cleaned her room in such a *slipshod* manner that it wasn't any neater after she finished.
slither v slith-er: to slide
The kids *slithered* down the vine into the water.
sliver n sliv-er: splinter
A *sliver* of wood was stuck in her hand.
sliver v sliv-er: to cut or split into slivers
He *slivered* the meat into several slices.
slouch v slouch: to droop, bend downward
She *slouched* in her seat although she had been warned to sit up properly.
slovenly adj slov-en-ly: untidy, sloppy
Although he owns several nice suits, he prefers to dress in a *slovenly* way.
sluggish adj slug-gish: slow moving
His *sluggish* walking suggests that he received too little sleep last night.
slump v slump: to drop, fall, decline
The doll *slumped* down on the floor of the closet.

slump n slump: a sudden fall
A *slump* of activity in the office left employees with nothing to do.
slur v slur: to pronounce indistinctly, slide over
He *slurred* his speech so badly that we could not understand what he was saying.
slur n slur: connecting notes
The correct way to write that music is with a *slur* between the first and second notes.
smite v smite: to hit hard, strike
If you *smite* him one more time, I will notify the officers to take him away from you.
smother v smoth-er: to deprive of air
Open a window before we *smother* in here.
smudge v smudge: to smear, streak with dirt
The child *smudged* his outfit with mud.
smudge n smudge: a dirty spot
All the scrubbing in the world would not remove the *smudge* from his shirt.
snag n snag: hidden obstacle, a sharp point or projection
A *snag* in the thread prevented him from sewing any further.
snag v snag: to damage on a snag
She *snagged* her nylons against the nail protruding from the fence.
snarl n snarl: growl
The dog emitted a menacing *snarl* when the stranger approached.
snarl v snarl: tangle, or cause to be tangled
The dog twisted around so many times that she became *snarled* in her leash.
snicker n snick-er: giggle, laugh
A *snicker* escaped her lips even while her mother was scolding her.
snub v snub: to treat coldly
She was bewildered when some of her new classmates *snubbed* her.
snub adj snub: short, turned up
Their baby is so cute with her large eyes and *snub* nose.
snug adj snug: comfortable, sheltered
He preferred to stay in his *snug* bed rather than face the morning cold air.
soar v soar: to fly high, rise
The birds *soared* above the farm.
sob v sob: to cry
The kids *sobbed* when their friends went away for the holidays.
sob n sob: the act or sound of crying
They heard a *sob* from the child when she realized that she was alone in the room.

sober adj so-ber: not drunk, serious
Don't let him drive the car until he is *sober* again.
The professor had a *sober* expression on his face.

sober v so-ber: to make or become sober
A cold shower *sobered* her up enough in the morning to report to work on time.

sociable adj so-cia-ble: friendly
His *sociable* manner has made him very popular here.

sodden adj sod-den: soaked
They packed up their *sodden* belongings after the rainstorm.

soggy adj sog-gy: heavy with moisture
Although the air was warm, the grass was still too *soggy* to walk across.

solace n sol-ace: comfort, relief
He sought *solace* from his mother when he hurt his foot.

solace v sol-ace: to comfort, to console
She *solaced* her son when he ran in crying.

solar adj so-lar: of the sun
Their house is warmed naturally with *solar* heat.

sole adj sole: one and only, exclusive
He was the *sole* guest who showed for the dinner.

solemn adj sol-emn: serious, grave
This is going to be a *solemn* affair.

solicit v so-lic-it: to beg, ask for
She *solicited* her parents for the money to pay for her car.

solicitude n so-lic-i-tude: state of anxiety, concerned
The teacher had great *solicitude* for the welfare of her students.

soliloquy n so-lil-o-quy: monologue
He delivered a witty *soliloquy* to the delighted audience.

somber adj som-ber: gloomy, dark
A *somber* look appeared on his face when he read the bad news.

sonnet n son-net: fourteen line poem
Their assignment was to write a *sonnet* and read it to the class.

sonorous adj so-no-rous: rich, resonant sound
His *sonorous* voice was the cause of his success.

soothe v soothe: calm down, comfort
Her soft, quiet voice *soothed* his fears.

soothsayer n sooth-sayer: predictor
The *soothsayer* told him that he would be sent on a voyage next year.

sorcerer n sor-cer-er: magician
Children and adults alike were fascinated by the tricks performed by the *sorcerer*.

sordid adj sor-did: dirty, filthy
I can't understand how he can continue to live in such *sordid* *conditions*.

souse v souse: to pickle
She *soused* the garden vegetables in vinegar.

souse n souse: a drenching, soaking
A *souse* of water and epsom salts will reduce the swelling in his foot.

souvenir n sou-ve-nir: keepsake
She kept the program as a *souvenir* of the performance she had just seen.

sovereign n sov-er-eign: ruler, monarch
As *sovereign* of the tiny country, he governs his countrymen with wisdom.

sovereign adj sov-er-eign: above all others, chief, supreme
Her *sovereign* position in the office grants her final approval power over all decisions.

sow n sow: female pig
The *sow* escaped her pen and roamed in the garden behind the house.

sow v sow: to plant seed
They cleared the land so that they could *sow* in time for a summer garden of fresh vegetables.

spacious adj spa-cious: vast, roomy
They were not used to living in such *spacious* quarters.

spade n spade: shovel
Use a *spade* to dig that tree out of the garden.

spade v spade: to dig with a spade
Carefully *spade* the flowers out of this row.

span n span: distance between
There is a *span* of twenty years from the time this house was built until it was renovated.

span v span: to measure, especially by the span of the hand
They *spanned* the distance between the walls.

sparse adj sparse: scanty, meager
Unfortunately, there is only a *sparse* selection of canned foods left in the cupboard.

specific adj spe-cif-ic: definite, precise
His *specific* instructions were to turn right at the corner.

specific n spe-cif-ic: a particular case
The *specifics* stated that we should not enter that house.

spectacles n spec-ta-cles: glasses
They wore *spectacles* to protect their eyes from the sunlight.

spectator n spec-ta-tor: viewer
Several *spectators* told the police what had happened.

specter n spec-ter: ghost
A *specter* appeared at the top of the stairs of the old house.

spigot n spig-ot: valve, faucet
He hooked up a *spigot* to the outside wall so that they could draw water for the garden.

spinster n spin-ster: old maid
The *spinster* lives alone in her large house.

spiritual adj spir-it-u-al: sacred, religious
A *spiritual* ceremony is held here every Sunday night.

spiritual n spir-it-u-al: a religious folksong of American Negro origin
His favorite type of music is *spirituals*.

splice v splice: to join together
Splice that remaining tape on to this new roll.

splice n splice: a joint made by splicing
This is the *splice* at which he merged the ropes.

spontaneous adj spon-ta-ne-ous: not planned
The *spontaneous* concert drew a large crowd.

sprawl v sprawl: to spread out
The cats *sprawled* on the rug in front of the warm fireplace.

sprawl n sprawl: a sprawling movement or position
He meant to dive into the pool head first, but he hit the water in a *sprawl*.

spree n spree: lively frolic
A *spree* of activity broke out as soon as the children were released from their classes.

sprig n sprig: twig, small branch
A *sprig* from a maple tree floated in the pool.

sprightly adj spright-ly: lively, gay
A *sprightly* group of elderly men and women danced for hours.

sprint v sprint: to run fast
She *sprinted* to the finish line in record-breaking time.

sprint n sprint: fast run
Seeing that he was losing time, he broke into a *sprint*.

sprite n sprite: elf, fairy
It is rumored that a *sprite* lives in the forest.

sprout v sprout: to grow
The seeds you planted last fall are *sprouting* now.

sprout n sprout: a young growth on a plant
The arrival of spring brought about several new green *sprouts* on the tree.

spry adj spry: active, lively
Her *spry* motions surprised the guard, who thought she was asleep.
spurious adj spu-ri-ous: false
A *spurious* sense of panic overtook him when he thought that his house was on fire.
spurn v spurn: to refuse
He *spurned* her invitation for dinner because he had already made other plans.
spurt v spurt: to gush, squirt
When she shook the bottle, the cap flew off and water *spurted* all over the floor.
spurt n spurt: a brief, sudden effort
All I need is one more *spurt* of energy to get this job done.
squalid adj squal-id: filthy
When he moved out, he left the apartment in a *squalid* condition.
squall n squall: violent windstorm
A *squall* hit the resort town and ruined the weekend for the tourists.
squander v squan-der: to waste
She *squandered* her wealth away foolishly.
squash v squash: to crush
The fallen tree *squashed* the garden.
squash n squash: a game played with rackets; a fleshy fruit
Their favorite evening activity is to play *squash*.
The *squash* is a relative of the pumpkin.
squat v squat: to crouch
They *squatted* behind the furniture so that they could surprise him when he arrived.
squat adj squat: short and heavy or thick
The *squat* dog ambled slowly down the path.
squat n squat: the position of squatting
She bent in a *squat* while doing her gardening.
squelch v squelch: to crush
The trash compacter *squelched* the leftovers into tiny piles.
squelch n squelch: a crushing retort
He replied to her rude question with a *squelch*.
stabilize v sta-bi-lize: to make firm, steady
Stabilize the sign by bracing it up against this pole.
staff n staff: stick, pole, rod; a group of people
She leaned against the *staff* as she hobbled down the road.
The boss was kind to his *staff*.
stag n stag: male deer
The *stag* bent to drink out of the brook.

stag adv stag: unaccompanied by a date
The invitation requests that you attend *stag*.

stagnant adj stag-nant: not active
The odor remained in the *stagnant* air for several hours.

stale adj stale: not fresh
The bread that was left out over night is now *stale*.

stale v stale: to become dry or flat
That cereal will *stale* if you don't cover it.

stallion n stal-lion: male horse
That horse is the finest *stallion* at the race.

stalwart adj stal-wart: strong, brave
He defended his family with a *stalwart* stance.

stamina n stam-i-na: endurance
He built up his *stamina* for the race by jogging every morning.

stammer v stam-mer: to stutter
She was so frightened that she *stammered* out her account of what had happened.

stammer n stam-mer: a stutter
Even though she speaks with a *stammer*, she sings without a trace of difficulty.

stampede n stam-pede: sudden scattering
The loud, unexpected noise sent the flock into a *stampede*.

stampede v stam-pede: to move in a stampede
The herd of buffalo *stampeded* across the prairie.

stanchion n stan-chion: bar, post
The horses were tethered to the *stanchion*.

startle v star-tle: to surprise, frighten
He was *startled* to see several of his friends waiting for him in his house.

stationary adj sta-tion-ary: still, not moving
He stood in a *stationary* position for several minutes.

stationery n sta-tion-ery: paper
Write your letter on the company's *stationery*.

stature n stat-ure: height
The new building will have a *stature* of one hundred stories.

status n sta-tus: condition, rank
Her *status* in the office improved when she completed the job in a short time.

steed n steed: horse
That animal is the finest *steed* in the county.

steep adj steep: sharp slope
The *steep* path prevented them from climbing any further with all their gear.

stench n stench: bad smell, stink
Those fumes left a *stench* in the air.

sterile adj ster-ile: germ free, barren
The newborn infants were kept in a *sterile* room.

stern adj stern: severe, strict
A *stern* expression appeared on her face when she disciplined her children.

stern n stern: rear end of a boat
Be sure that you balance the weight in the boat by having someone sit in the *stern* as well.

stevedore n ste-ve-dore: unloader
Stevedores waited near the tracks for the freight train to arrive with its cargo.

stifle v sti-fle: to suppress, smother
She *stifled* her desire to show the child the way since she knew it was better if he tried it alone.

stigma n stig-ma: stain, disgrace
His behavior left a *stigma* on his family's good name.

stilted adj stilt-ed: formal, dignified
She spoke to the crowd in a *stilted* manner.

stimulate v stim-u-late: to stir up, rouse
The clowns will appear first to *stimulate* the audience to laughter.

stingy adj stin-gy: not generous
She was *stingy* with her portions of the dessert.

stipend n sti-pend: salary
She pays her rent out of her monthly *stipend*.

stocky adj stock-y: solid, sturdy
All that excess food has given him a *stocky* build.

stoic adj sto-ic: self-controlled
His *stoic* ability to oversee the project soon put everybody at ease.

stoke v stoke: to stir up
Stoke the fire with this prong to get it burning again.

stout adj stout: fat and large
She was so *stout* that she could not fit into the chair.

stow v stow: to pack
Stow the summer gear away for the winter months.

straggle v strag-gle: to wander, stray
The chickens *straggled* across the yard after she left the hen house open.

strenuous adj stren-u-ous: very active
The *strenuous* workout left them huffing and puffing.

stress n stress: pressure, strain

The *stress* of doing two jobs at one time was too great for them to handle.

stress v stress: to put pressure on
You will *stress* the sofa too much if you continue to jump around on it.

strew v strew: to scatter, sprinkle
The falling leaves were *strewn* across the park.

strident adj stri-dent: harsh sounding
She had a *strident* voice that annoyed everyone.

strife n strife: quarrel, fight
Their *strife* was over the use of the equipment.

strive v strive: to try hard
They *strive* to climb the mountain every year.

stroll n stroll: leisurely walk
They enjoy a *stroll* through the woods each evening after dinner.

stroll v stroll: to walk about leisurely
Many people *stroll* along the beach instead of swimming.

structure n struc-ture: building, arrangement
The city plans to build several more *structures* on the waterfront next year.

stucco n stuc-co: plaster
They reinforced the wall with *stucco*.

stun v stun: to daze, bewilder
The surprise arrival of her parents *stunned* her.

stupefy v stu-pe-fy: to astound, stun
His amazing feats of daring *stupefied* the audience.

stupor n stu-por: dazed condition
A *stupor* came over him as he stared out of the window.

sturdy adj stur-dy: robust, strong, firm
His *sturdy* build made him very popular with the women.

stymie v sty-mie: to block completely
The accident at the corner *stymied* traffic in all directions.

suave adj suave: gracious, polite
They were impressed with his *suave* manners.

subdue v sub-due: to overcome, conquer
She *subdued* her fears and faced the crowd.

sublime adj sub-lime: noble, majestic
They were impressed by his *sublime* mannerisms and assumed that he was the head of the house.

subpoena n sub-poe-na: writ summoning a witness
They issued a *subpoena* to the man who saw the accident.

subsequent adj sub-se-quent: following, after
Any *subsequent* reports should be filed behind this one.

subside v sub-side: to grow less
The storm *subsided* during the night and the sun was shining by morning.

subtle adj sub-tle: delicate, elusive
The *subtle* aroma of his cologne remained in the room after he had left.

subvert v sub-vert: to ruin, overthrow
He will *subvert* all their careful planning by his actions.

succinct adj suc-cinct: concise, brief
They want us to turn in the *succinct* report of the events at the meeting.

succulent adj suc-cu-lent: juicy
The *succulent* steak made her mouth water in hunger.

succumb v suc-cumb: yield, give in to
She *succumbed* to his persistent request to go out with him.

suffice v suf-fice: to be enough, satisfy a need
This first draft will *suffice* for now, but please have the final draft completed by Friday.

suffrage n suf-frage: voting
Woman's *suffrage* is increasing each year.

sulk v sulk: be sullen, aloof
She *sulked* in her room after her father told her that she could not buy that coat.

sullen adj sul-len: gloomy, dismal
A *sullen* sky spoiled their plans for a picnic today.

sultry adj sul-try: hot and moist
The *sultry* weather prevented anyone from wanting to play any sports outdoors.

summit n sum-mit: the top, acme
They reached the *summit* of the hill and then started the long decline.

sumptuous adj sump-tu-ous: magnificent
They always serve a *sumptuous* Thanksgiving dinner.

sundry adj sun-dry: various, several
Sundry items were for sale at the store.

superfluous adj su-per-flu-ous: more than needed
Put any *superfluous* materials into the storage closet.

superlative adj su-per-la-tive: supreme
The *superlative* compliment you can give him is friendship.

supersede v su-per-sede: to replace
The assistant *superseded* the boss when he went away.

supine adj su-pine: lying flat
The cat stretched out in a *supine* position on the sofa.

supplant v sup-plant: to displace, set aside
The computer *supplanted* the job previously done by three people.
supple adj sup-ple: bending easily
The old man could not keep up with the *supple* youth in the race to complete the job.
supplement n sup-ple-ment: addition
A *supplement* to the newspaper will be included in this week's paper.
supplement v sup-ple-ment: to fill up the deficiencies of, add to
You should *supplement* your diet with vitamin pills.
suppress v sup-press: to stop, put an end to
He *suppressed* his desire to eat another piece of candy and drank some water instead.
supreme adj su-preme: utmost, highest
He received the *supreme* honor for his bravery.
surfeit n sur-feit: excess
They received a *surfeit* of supplies.
surfeit v sur-feit: to overindulge
You will spoil that child if you continue to *surfeit* him with anything he wants.
surge v surge: to rise and fall
Waves *surged* on the rugged coastline, sending a fine mist into the air.
surge n surge: a large billow, increase in current
A *surge* of people gathered to hear the concert.
surmise n sur-mise: guess
His *surmise* is that they will arrive around noon.
surmise v sur-mise: to guess
She *surmised* that there was a sweater in the box.
surname n sur-name: family name
She prefers to use her *surname* to her husband's last name.
surpass v sur-pass: to exceed
He *surpassed* her efforts and set a new record.
surplus n sur-plus: excess, extra
The *surplus* of equipment was sent back to the office.
surrogate n sur-ro-gate: substitute
A *surrogate* will be found for your class until your teacher can return.
surveillance n sur-veil-lance: watch over
A *surveillance* was set up during the month that the paintings were on display at the museum.
survey v sur-vey: to inspect, examine
They *surveyed* the damage left in the cellar when the pipes broke and flooded.

survey n sur-vey: a general study, as by sampling opinion
A *survey* of the residents proved that they were in favor of having a shopping mall nearby.

survive v sur-vive: to outlive, remain alive
At ninety years old, she had *survived* her brothers and sisters.

suspend v sus-pend: to hang from above; stop for awhile
The decorations were *suspended* from the ceiling beams.
The boy's television privileges were *suspended*.

sustain v sus-tain: to support, maintain
Her friends *sustained* her throughout the ordeal.

swagger v swag-ger: to sway, strut
After winning the award, he *swaggered* from the auditorium.

swagger n swag-ger: swaggering walk or manner
He walked down the aisle in a *swagger*.

swarm n swarm: crowd
A *swarm* of bees buzzed over their heads.

swarm v swarm: to fly off in a swarm, to move
The mosquitoes *swarmed* over the unprotected tourists.

swelter v swel-ter: to suffer from heat
She *sweltered* in the sunlight.

swelter n swel-ter: oppressive heat
Nobody wants to participate until this *swelter* is over.

swerve v swerve: to turn aside
The vehicles *swerved* to the right to avoid the obstacle in the road.

swerve n swerve: a swerving
A sudden *swerve* of the wheels sent the truck careening off the road into the ditch.

swine n swine: pigs, hogs
They raise *swine* as well as cattle on this farm.

swirl v swirl: to twist, whirl
The flag *swirled* in the wind.

swoon v swoon: to faint
He frightened her so much that she *swooned*.

swoon n swoon: a faint
She collapsed onto the floor in a *swoon*.

sycamore n syc-a-more: shade tree
Their favorite meeting place is under the giant *sycamore* in the center of the park.

sylvan adj syl-van: woodsy
The *sylvan* view from their back window is lovely.

symmetry n sym-me-try: balanced arrangement
He wants *symmetry* in this room, so move that chair up to the same level as this one.

sympathy n sym-pa-thy: sharing of sorrow
They all felt *sympathy* for her loss.
symposium n sym-po-si-um: meeting for discussion of a subject
They held a *symposium* on the subject of security.
synthetic adj syn-thet-ic: artificial
The *synthetic* fur coat looks just as attractive as the real fur coat.

T

tabloid n tab-loid: newspaper
He reads the daily *tabloid* at breakfast.
taboo n ta-boo: forbidden, banned
Those words are *taboo* here.
taboo adj ta-boo: prohibited or restricted by
Politics is a *taboo* subject at our meetings.
taboo v ta-boo: to prohibit
The officials *tabooed* their wishes to go swimming in the pond.
tabulate v tab-u-late: to list, arrange
Tabulate the contributions into separate categories according to quality.
tacit adj tac-it: silent, unspoken
They nodded their heads in *tacit* agreement from opposite ends of the room.
tactile adj tac-tile: via sense of touch
The plant is so sensitive to *tactile* encounters that it is placed safely out of reach.
tadpole n tad-pole: young frog
The boys went searching for a *tadpole* to add to their collection in the pond.
taint v taint: to affect with something unpleasant
The fire *tainted* our view of the woods.
taint n taint: a trace of contamination, corruption
The *taint* of their ideas spoiled the event.
talisman n tal-is-man: magic charm
She is so superstitious that she always carries a *talisman* with her.
tangent n tan-gent: a curve, line or surface touching another line without intersecting
They painted a *tangent* line on the surface of the road.

tangible adj tan-gi-ble: definite; real
The criminal left *tangible* evidence of his crime.
tankard n tank-ard: drinking mug
They served his beer in a *tankard*.
tantamount adj tan-ta-mount: equivalent
His statement was *tantamount* to a confession.
taper v ta-per: to gradually decrease
The rain *tapered* to a fine mist and then stopped completely.
taper n ta-per: a slender candle
She lit the *taper* on the table for dinner.
tardy adj tar-dy: late
I missed the lecture because I was *tardy* in arriving.
tariff n tar-iff: tax
A *tariff* will be applied to your merchandise.
tarnish v tar-nish: to dull the luster of
Scraping the furniture across the floor *tarnished* its surface.
tarnish n tar-nish: dullness, less coloration, stain
Constant abuse to the floor left a *tarnish* on it that could not be removed.
tarry v tar-ry: to remain
They *tarried* in the theater long after the show had ended.
tart n tart: pastry
For breakfast, she prefers hot chocolate and a cinnamon *tart*.
tart adj tart: sharp, sour
The soured milk left a *tart* taste in the casserole.
tattered adj tat-tered: torn and ragged
It is time that you replace that *tattered* rug.
taunt v taunt: to mock, jeer
The children *taunted* the gorilla's actions.
taunt n taunt: scornful or jeering remark
She answered his impertinent question with a *taunt*.
taut adj taut: tight
He fastened the boat to the pier with a *taut* rope.
tawdry adj taw-dry: showy, cheap
She wore a *tawdry* outfit to the theater.
tease v tease: to annoy, vex; to raise a nap
The boy *teased* his sister unceasingly.
She *teased* the blue velvet with her hand.
tease n tease: a teasing or being teased
No one takes him seriously because he is such a *tease*.
tedious adj te-di-ous: monotonous
The *tedious* task of counting all those receipts seemed endless.

teem v teem: to be full of
The train station *teemed* with people rushing to catch their trains.
temerity n te-mer-i-ty: boldness, rashness
She faced her parents with *temerity* in making her announcement.
tempest n tem-pest: storm, disturbance
Warnings of a *tempest* blowing in from sea sent the tourists running for cover.
tenacious adj te-na-cious: fierce, stubborn
A *tenacious* wind gripped the boat and turned it over.
tendency n tend-en-cy: trend, inclination
Her *tendency* is to have a hot cup of tea each evening after dinner.
tenement n ten-e-ment: dwelling
Their *tenement* is on the corner.
tense adj tense: nervous, stretched tight
There was a *tense* mood throughout the room.
tense v tense: to make or become tense
He *tensed* his muscles in an attempt to feel warmer in the snow.
tense n tense: any form of a verb that shows time of action
The *tense* for that word should be in the future.
tepid adj tep-id: lukewarm
He prefers to shower in *tepid* water.
terrestrial adj ter-res-tri-al: earthly
Some areas of the moon appear *terrestrial*.
terse adj terse: brief
She yelled out a *terse* reply as she ran by.
thaw v thaw: to melt, become warmer
The snow *thawed* in the warm air.
thaw n thaw: a warm spell to permit melting
Ships cannot pass through this channel until after the spring *thaw*.
theme n theme: topic, subject
The *theme* of his paper is about Russia.
theorem n the-o-rem: rule
That math *theorem* states that one should divide the sum.
therapy n ther-a-py: treatment of diseases
This institution provides excellent *therapy* to all its patients.
thermal adj ther-mal: warm, hot
Cover the baby with a *thermal* blanket.
thrall n thrall: slave
She complains that she feels like a *thrall* to the kitchen.
thrash v thrash: to beat
Thrash the rug with this broom to get that dirt out.
threshold n thresh-old: doorway

They request that we leave our boots at the *threshold* before entering the room.

thrift n thrift: saving
Their *thrift* resulted in a considerable amount of money at the end of the year.

thrive v thrive: to grow, prosper
The flowers *thrived* in the afternoon sun.

throb v throb: to tremble, quiver
The dog's tail *throbbed* excitedly when he saw that she was bringing his meal.

throb n throb: a throbbing strong beat or pulsation
The *throb* of pain in her head continued throughout the evening.

throng n throng: crowd, multitude
A *throng* of thousands lined the streets to view the passing cavalcade.

throng v throng: to crowd into
They *thronged* into the only bus to come along in an hour.

thud n thud: dull sound, thump
The sign landed with a *thud* on the ground.

thwart v thwart: block, defeat
He *thwarted* her attempts to reach the finish line first.

tidbit n tid-bit: morsel of food
She will get sick if she continues to consume only *tidbits*.

tidings n ti-dings: information
They drive into town once a week to hear all the neighborly *tidings*.

tier n tier: row
A *tier* of seats has been reserved for your group.

tiff n tiff: a little quarrel
They seldom fight, but sometimes they have a *tiff*.

till v till: to cultivate, plow
He *tilled* the land for the new crops.

till n till: a drawer for keeping money
Get his allowance out of the *till*.

timid adj tim-id: shy
The *timid* child hid behind his mother when the guests arrived.

timorous adj tim-or-ous: fearful
He spoke to his grandfather in a *timorous* voice.

tirade n ti-rade: long scolding speech
Their father delivered a *tirade* to his delinquent children.

titanic adj ti-tan-ic: gigantic, vast
Some people think of the city as a *titanic* hunk of concrete and steel.

toga n to-ga: robe, garment
She covered her swimsuit with a warm *toga*.

toil v toil: to work, labor
He *toiled* hour after hour in the garage until the engine was fixed.

token n to-ken: sign, keepsake
Their embraces are a *token* of their love for each other.

token adj to-ken: merely simulated
His *token* sympathy didn't convince her that he cared.

tolerate v tol-er-ate: endure
She was not able to *tolerate* his screams.

toll n toll: tax, fee
You'll have to pay a *toll* before crossing the bridge.

toll v toll: to ring a bell
The church bells *tolled* the wedding music.

toll n toll: the sound of a bell ringing
The *toll* of Christmas music came out of the church.

tomb n tomb: grave, mausoleum
All their ancestors are buried in the *tomb*.

tomfoolery n tom-fool-er-y: nonsense
She was becoming annoyed at his persistent *tomfoolery*.

topple v top-ple: to fall, overturn
The statue *toppled* onto the sidewalk from the strong wind.

toreador n tor-e-a-dor: bullfighter
One of the tourist attractions in Spain is to watch the *toreador* challenge the bulls.

torment v tor-ment: to cause great pain
The continuous pounding in her head *tormented* her.

torment n tor-ment: a great pain
Her *torment* is the result of her fall on the ice.

tornado n tor-na-do: whirlwind
A *tornado* swept over the fair, leaving a path of debris behind.

torpid adj tor-pid: dull, inactive
A *torpid* mood seemed to come over everyone.

torrent n tor-rent: violent rush of water
The split in the dam sent a *torrent* of water racing down the mountain.

torrid adj tor-rid: very hot
She burned her hands when she submerged them in the *torrid* water.

tortoise n tor-toise: sea turtle
At the aquarium you will see a *tortoise* basking in the sun or swimming.

totter v tot-ter: to shake, be unsteady
The heavy object *tottered* on the flimsy stand.

toxic adj tox-ic: poisonous
Toxic fumes escaped from the laboratory.

trachea n tra-che-a: windpipe
Some food was caught in his *trachea*.

tract n tract: area of land or water
The *tract* extended for several miles in each direction from the farm.

tractable adj trac-ta-ble: easily managed
The drugged dart made the lion more *tractable*.

trait n trait: characteristic
One of his most interesting *traits* is his preference for all types of music.

trample v tram-ple: to crush
The child *trampled* the candy into the rug.

trample n tram-ple: the sound of trampling
A *trample* of hoofs was heard on the pavement.

trance n trance: dazed condition
All that loud noise and ceaseless activity has left him in a *trance*.

tranquil adj tran-quil: calm, peaceful
After the crowds left, a *tranquil* silence was all that remained.

transaction n trans-ac-tion: deal
They signed a *transaction* with the landlord to rent the apartment.

transcript n tran-script: copy, reproduction
She asked him for a *transcript* of his book.

transform v trans-form: to change, switch
Her Halloween costume *transformed* her into a witch.

transgress v trans-gress: to break a law
Samson *transgressed* the laws of his people.

transient adj tran-sient: not staying long
They will only be here for a *transient* visit.

transient n tran-sient: a homeless person
The boarding house on the corner caters to *transients*.

transition n tran-si-tion: change
There will be a *transition* in office policy starting next week.

transmit v trans-mit: to pass along
They *transmitted* the message from one person to another until it reached the other end.

transpire v tran-spire: to take place
Many events *transpired* over the weekend.

transport v trans-port: to carry
The moving van *transported* their furniture from their old house to their new residence.

transport n trans-port: in transportation
A *transport* of merchandise should arrive tomorrow.

transverse adj trans-verse: across
That route is *transverse* to the main road.

trauma n trau-ma: · physical or mental ill
The accident left him with a *trauma*.

travail n tra-vail: difficult labor
Years of *travail* were required before he became the head of the company.

travesty n trav-es-ty: imitation
That painting is a *travesty* of the real masterpiece in the museum.

treacherous adj treach-er-ous: disloyal
He lost all his friends following his *treacherous* actions.

tread v tread: to walk, step, trample
They *tread* softly outside the baby's room.

tread n tread: something upon which a person or thing walks
Each morning they walk the dog on the *tread* outside their apartment.

treason n trea-son: betrayal
His *treason* of his family was greeted with shocked disbelief.

trek n trek: journey, trip
They planned a *trek* across Canada that would last three months.

trek v trek: to travel or migrate arduously
The pioneers will *trek* across barren land before reaching their destination in the spring.

trench n trench: long narrow ditch
Move the debris out of the road and into the *trench*.

trench v trench: to dig a ditch
A crew *trenched* alongside the new highway.

trenchant adj tren-chant: sharp, effective
His *trenchant* comments offended the hostess.

trepidation n trep-i-da-tion: fear, apprehension
She approached the closed door with *trepidation*.

triad n tri-ad: group of three
They were divided into a *triad* for the experiment.

tribulation n trib-u-la-tion: great trouble
The settlers faced many *tribulations* during the early days of America.

tribunal n tri-bu-nal: court
The *tribunal* will meet tomorrow to decide what to do about the issue.

trident n tri-dent: three-pronged spear
He fishes with a *trident*.

trifle n tri-fle: small amount
A *trifle* of ice cream remains in the freezer for you.

tripod n tri-pod: three-legged stand
Place the camera on the *tripod*.

trite adj trite: worn out by use
Avoid relying on *trite* expressions when you write your book.

trivial adj triv-i-al: unimportant
That information is *trivial* and should be omitted.

truant n tru-ant: one who avoids duty
The *truants* play in the park rather than show up for class.

truce n truce: peace
The conflict was settled and the troops declared a *truce*.

truculent adj truc-u-lent: fierce, cruel
Her *truculent* treatment of the dog was unnecessary.

trudge v trudge: to walk heavily
He *trudged* up five flights of stairs with his laundry.

truncate v trun-cate: to cut off
The phone conversation was *truncated* when the telephone wire snapped.

truncheon n trun-cheon: policeman's club
They used their *truncheons* to disperse the crowd.

truss v truss: to bind, fasten
The leash was *trussed* to the fence so that the dog could not run too far.

truss n truss: a bundle or pack
The peasant threw his *truss* on his back and laboriously made his way down the path.

tryst n tryst: appointment, meeting
They arranged a *tryst* for next Sunday.

tumble v tum-ble: to fall
The rocks *tumbled* down the mountainside.

tumble n tum-ble: a fall, disorder
She is in the hospital with a broken leg because of the *tumble* she took from the building.

tunic n tu-nic: garment
He designed and sewed the *tunic* she is wearing.

turbine n tur-bine: engine
The *turbine* for the airplane is built in this warehouse.

turbulent adj tur-bu-lent: unruly, violent, disorderly
The *turbulent* classroom met with disapproval from the principal.

tureen n tu-reen: deep dish
Serve the soup in the *tureen*.

turf n turf: grass, sod, peat
They were warned to stay off the *turf* in the back yard.

turf v turf: to cover with turf
Their yard took such a beating from the storm that they plan to *turf* it again.

turgid adj tur-gid: swollen
The *turgid* condition of her ankle led us to believe that she had strained it.

turmoil n tur-moil: commotion
Her unexpected arrival created a *turmoil* at the office.

tusk n tusk: projecting tooth
The wild boar used its *tusk* as a weapon.

tutelage n tu-te-lage: act as teacher or guardian
He developed into a fine actor under his father's *tutelage*.

tutor n tu-tor: private teacher
She was having such difficulty with her math that she sought extra help from a *tutor*.

twig n twig: small branch
A *twig* from the tree broke off and landed in the water.

twine n twine: strong string or thread
Tie the package with *twine* after taping it down securely in all corners.

twine v twine: to twist together, weave
She *twined* the flowers into a necklace and placed it around her neck.

twinge n twinge: sudden, sharp pain
He felt a *twinge* of pain when the hot iron touched his arm.

twirl v twirl: to revolve, spin
She *twirled* the baton in dazzling speed.

twirl n twirl: a spinning
A *twirl* of wind scattered the newspaper in all directions.

tycoon n ty-coon: important businessman
This restaurants caters to clerks and *tycoons* alike.

tyke n tyke: mischievous child
The little *tyke* annoyed everyone at the table.

typhoon n ty-phoon: storm, tempest
People were forbidden to go near the ocean until the *typhoon* was over.

typical adj typ-i-cal: representative
We were not surprised when he gave us his *typical* reply.

tyrant n ty-rant: cruel ruler, despot
The citizens rebelled against the treatment they were receiving from the *tyrant*.

tyro n ty-ro: beginner, novice
He is a *tyro* at business, but he already shows a knack for it.

U

ultimate adj ul-ti-mate: final, utmost, maximum
Please let us know your *ultimate* decision by tomorrow.

umbrage n um-brage: resentment
She took *umbrage* at his unpleasant attitude.

uncanny adj un-can-ny: strange and mysterious
He has this *uncanny* way of knowing what I am going to say before I say it.

undaunted adj un-daunt-ed: not frightened
He entered the haunted house in an *undaunted* manner.

undulate v un-du-late: to move in waves
The field of grain *undulated* in the wind.

unerring adj un-err-ing: exactly right
His *unerring* answer was amazing since he was only guessing.

ungainly adj un-gain-ly: clumsy, awkward
The colt was still *ungainly* compared to his mother.

uniform adj u-ni-form: regular, same
He performs his job with *uniform* ease after all these years.

uniform v u-ni-form: to supply with a uniform
They *uniformed* all their employees in protective gear.

uniform n u-ni-form: distinctive clothes of a particular group
The *uniform* worn by all their students consists of white blouses and black slacks.

unify v u-ni-fy: to unite
The two teams *unified* their efforts and completed the task in half the time.

unique adj u-nique: one of a kind
She is envied by her friends for her *unique* job.

unison n u-ni-son: agreement
Approval was heard in *unison* from every member of the board of directors.

unity n uni-ty: oneness
A *unity* was felt among the gathered friends.

unkempt adj un-kempt: untidy
His room always appears in an *unkempt* condition.

unpalatable adj un-pal-at-a-ble: distasteful
They refused to eat the *unpalatable* seafood.

unravel v un-rav-el: to take apart
The sweater *unravelled* when the yarn got caught on the wire.

upbraid v up-braid: to reproach, condemn
He *upbraided* his son for his poor grades.

uproarious adj up-roar-i-ous: noisy and disorderly
His *uproarious* conduct at the meeting resulted in his being banned from any future gatherings.

upshot n up-shot: result
The *upshot* of the meeting is that you will be named to the committee.

urbane adj ur-bane: smoothly polite, polished
He is an *urbane* gentleman and admired by many people.

urchin n ur-chin: poor, ragged child
Although he appears to be an *urchin*, he is actually quite well off.

urge v urge: to solicit, entreat, impel
She *urged* her parents to buy the luggage for their trip.

urge n urge: an urging, an impulse
I have an *urge* to eat Chinese food.

urn n urn: vase
They place the bouquet of flowers in the *urn*.

usher v ush-er: to escort in, conduct
He *ushered* his mother into the church.

usher n ush-er: an official door keeper
Her arrival was announced by the *usher*.

usurp v u-surp: to take possession of
His power was *usurped* by the new commander.

utensil n u-ten-sil: implement
She stocked her kitchen with new *utensils*.

utmost n ut-most: greatest possible
The *utmost* anyone can do is to try their best.

utmost adj ut-most: most extreme
She danced with the *utmost* energy for the audition.

utter adj ut-ter: complete, total
She had such a headache that her family left her in *utter* silence.

utter v ut-ter: to speak
He *uttered* the words she wanted to hear.

V

vaccinate v vac-ci-nate: to innoculate
The school board insists that all its students be *vaccinated* for measles before school starts.
vacillate v va-cil-late: to waver
The members continued to *vacillate* before the vote.
vacuum n vac-u-um: empty space, void
A *vacuum* was left where the house used to be.
vacuum v vac-u-um: to clean with a vacuum cleaner
The floor needs to be *vacuumed* after the meeting.
vagabond adj vag-a-bond: wanderer, vagrant
A *vagabond* camped out in the field last night before resuming his travels south.
vagrant n va-grant: wanderer
The *vagrant* slept in the hallways at night.
vagrant adj va-grant: following no fixed course, random
They traveled south in a *vagrant* style.
vague adj vague: not clear
Your answer is too *vague* for them to understand.
vain adj vain: unsuccessful
They made a *vain* attempt to lift the heavy suitcase.
valedictory adj val-e-dic-to-ry: pertaining to a farewell address
The graduates listened to a particularly interesting *valedictory* speech.
valiant adj val-iant: courageous
Her *valiant* actions will be rewarded.
valid adj val-id: true, sound
We need *valid* proof of your story.
valise n va-lise: luggage
He packed his *valise* for a weekend trip to the country.
valor n val-or: bravery, courage
He approached his foes with such *valor* that they backed away.
vanish v van-ish: to disappear
All the cookies she had baked last night had *vanished* by morning.
vanity n van-i-ty: pride
Her *vanity* was hurt when he insulted her appearance.
vapor n va-por: mist, fog
The *vapor* was so dense that he could not see far enough ahead to drive without lights.

variable adj var-i-a-ble: changeable
Their vacation plans are *variable* at this stage.

variation n var-i-a-tion: change
After months of following the same schedule, they looked forward to a *variation* in plans.

vassal n vas-sal: servant, slave
He was the king's *vassal*.

vast adj vast: immense
The *vast* size of the arena was more than they expected.

vault v vault: to leap, jump
The horse *vaulted* over the bushes.

vault n vault: cellar, safe place; vaulting, an arched roof
The money was hidden in the *vault*.
The tourists gazed in awe at the cloister *vault* above.

veer v veer: to change direction
The airplane *veered* off its course to avoid the thunderstorm.

veer n veer: a change of direction
A sharp *veer* to the left sent the passengers tumbling into the aisle.

vehement adj ve-he-ment: forceful, violent
His *vehement* denial surprised his family.

veil v veil: to cover
She *veiled* the birdcage with a light cloth to quiet the bird.

veil n veil: a piece of light fabric as of net
She never appears outdoors without a *veil* to protect her delicate skin.

velocity n ve-loc-i-ty: speed
He was pedaling his bike with such *velocity* that he could not stop at the corner.

vend v vend: to peddle, sell
To *vend* her merchandise, she had to send out a promotional letter.

vendetta n ven-det-ta: vengeful feud
He swore to end the *vendetta* between them.

veneer n ve-neer: covering
They reupholstered the sofa with a leather *veneer*.

veneer v ve-neer: to cover with a thin layer of something
The factory *veneered* the chipboard with a thin slice of walnut.

vengeance n ven-geance: revenge
He attacked the boy with *vengeance* for what had been done to his sister.

venison n ven-i-son: deer meat
Not everyone enjoys eating *venison*.

venom n ven-om: poison
The snake bite left *venom* in his body.

ventilate v ven-ti-late: to circulate fresh air; discuss freely
Open the window so that we can *ventilate* the room.
He *ventilated* his views freely.

venture n ven-ture: risky undertaking
In her business, one tries several *ventures* in a year.

venture v ven-ture: to take a risk
Venture a decision about which is the correct answer to the math problem.

verbatim adj ver-bat-im: word for word
His *verbatim* account of the accident was quite accurate.

verbose adj ver-bose: wordy
The *verbose* presentation bored the students.

verdant adj ver-dant: green
The forest was *verdant* and lush.

verdict n ver-dict: decision, judgment
The jury agreed on a guilty *verdict* for the offender.

verify v ver-if-y: to confirm
The hotel clerk *verified* their reservations for the weekend.

vermin n ver-min: small troublesome animals
They have to keep the trash containers tightly closed so as not to attract hungry *vermin*.

vernacular n ver-nac-u-lar: native language
I cannot understand what he says when he speaks in his *vernacular*.

versatile adj ver-sa-tile: many-sided abilities
All that training and education has given her a *versatile* background.

versus prep ver-sus: against
It was the green team *versus* the red team.

vertex n ver-tex: highest point, top
They climbed to the *vertex* of the mountain.

vertigo n ver-ti-go: dizziness
His *vertigo* makes it impossible for him to pilot the plane.

vessel n ves-sel: boat, ship
The *vessel* carried shipments of material across the ocean.

vestibule n ves-ti-bule: hallway
The house features a long *vestibule* from the front door to the living room.

veto v ve-to: to reject
She *vetoed* his suggestion to go away for the weekend.

veto n ve-to: a prohibiting order
Their suggestions for the campaign met with a *veto* from the head of the agency.

vex v vex: to anger, provoke, annoy

They *vexed* her to the point where she started yelling at them to leave.

via   prep   vi-a: by way of
They traveled to Canada *via* Michigan.

viaduct   n   vi-a-duct: bridge
A *viaduct* connected one township with another.

vial   n   vi-al: small bottle
He filled the *vial* with a sampling of the liquid.

vibrate   v   vi-brate: to move rapidly to and fro
The dishes *vibrated* in the cupboard while he was hammering.

vice   n   vice: evil habit, fault, defect
He considers smoking cigarettes to be his worst *vice*.

vicinity   n   vi-cin-i-ty: nearness
She was in the *vicinity* of her first house.

vicious   adj   vi-cious: wicked
The old man, who lives on the corner, has a *vicious* temper.

vie   v   vie: to compete, strive
Each of the contestants *vied* for first place.

vigilant   adj   vig-i-lant: alertly watchful
The dog sat in *vigilant* silence outside of his master's door.

vigor   n   vig-or: energy, power
He claims to get his *vigor* from those vitamin pills.

vile   adj   vile: wicked
His *vile* behavior landed him in jail.

vilify   v   vil-i-fy: to defame, slander
He attempted to *vilify* the politician.

villa   n   vil-la: house
They like to spend the summer months at their *villa* near the ocean.

vindicate   v   vin-di-cate: to defend, justify
She *vindicated* her friend against their accusations.

viper   n   vi-per: snake
A *viper* slithered in the tall grass beside the pond.

virile   adj   vir-ile: manly, masculine
The boy assumed a *virile* manner when he addressed the guests.

virtue   n   vir-tue: goodness
His *virtue* was rewarded with a trip to the farm.

virulent   adj   vir-u-lent: harmful
The *virulent* ingredient in the detergent was removed.

visa   n   vi-sa: passport
You will need to obtain a *visa* before traveling to those countries.

viscous   adj   vis-cous: thick
The *viscous* water seeped down the path.

vital adj vi-tal: necessary
Eggs are a *vital* ingredient in that recipe.

vitals n vi-tals: the vital organs: the heart, brain, etc.
They feared that the exposure to the cold air would harm his *vitals*.

vivid adj viv-id: bright, intense
The *vivid* sunlight flooded the room with illumination.

vocation n vo-ca-tion: occupation, career
He quit his writing job because he wished to change his *vocation* to business management.

vociferous adj vo-cif-er-ous: loud and noisy
The people at the rear table talked in *vociferous* tones that could be heard throughout the diner.

vogue n vogue: fashion, popularity
It is in *vogue* to wear your dress at knee length.

void n void: an empty space
The removal of the materials left a *void* in the container.

void v void: to make empty; render useless
The secretary *voided* her check.

volatile adj vol-a-tile: explosive, changeable, fickle
Her *volatile* temper often got her into trouble.

volition n vo-li-tion: willingness
He accepted our proposal of his own *volition*.

voluble adj vol-u-ble: talking too much
He tries to avoid her *voluble* conversations on the phone.

voracious adj vo-ra-cious: eating greedily
Following three days of fasting, their *voracious* attack on the food was understandable.

vortex n vor-tex: whirlpool
The combination of hot and cold winds created a *vortex* in the air.

vouch v vouch: to assert, affirm, attest
She *vouched* for his reliability.

vow n vow: promise
He made a *vow* to exercise every evening.

vow v vow: to promise or declare solemnly
They *vowed* to complete her job for her when she became ill.

vulgar adj vul-gar: coarse, unrefined
His *vulgar* language infuriated the hostess.

vulnerable adj vul-ner-a-ble: open to attack
The roof blew off the house, leaving the occupants *vulnerable* to the storm.

W

wade v wade: to walk through water
Following the storm, the kids *waded* through the puddles in the street.

wager v wag-er: to gamble, bet
He *wagered* that he would come in first in the race.

waif n waif: neglected child
The police took the *waif* to the orphanage.

wail v wail: to cry
The baby *wailed* for attention.

waive v waive: to relinquish
He *waived* his control of the stockroom and let them use it freely.

wallow v wal-low: to flounder, roll about
The fish *wallowed* on the beach where it had been washed up.

wallow n wal-low: an act of floundering
The *wallow* of the boat made them feel uneasy.

wan adj wan: pale
By the end of the cold season, they all had *wan* coloring on their faces from lack of sun.

wane v wane: to decline
His popularity *waned* over the years.

wanton adj wan-ton: reckless; heartless, lewd
He is denied use of the family car because of his *wanton* way of driving.
Salome was a *wanton* young girl.

warden n ward-en: keeper, guard
A *warden* is always on duty outside the prison.

warp n warp: a distortion
A *warp* in the record prevented them from playing it.

warp v warp: to bend, twist out of shape
The extreme heat *warped* the neck of the guitar.

warrant n war-rant: guarantee; authorization to make an arrest
The new product came with a *warrant* for service.
They issued a *warrant* for his arrest.

warrant v war-rant: to authorize
One of the officials must *warrant* your idea before we can put it into practice.

wary adj war-y: careful, cautious
They approached the cage with *wary* steps.

waver v wa-ver: to vary
His plans *wavered* when he received additional news.

wayfarer n way-far-er: traveler
A *wayfarer* stopped by the motel and inquired about rates for the night.

waylay v way-lay: to attack, rob
He feared that someone would *waylay* him on the road as he traveled with the valuable cargo.

wayward adj way-ward: disobedient
They sent their dog to training school to correct his *wayward* habits.

weep v weep: to cry
She began to *weep* when she won the contest.

weird adj weird: mysterious, unearthly
Neighbors gathered in the field to look at the *weird* object that had fallen from the sky.

weld v weld: to join together
He *welded* the typewriter to the desk so that no one could remove it.

weld n weld: joint made by welding
This *weld* will keep the stove in place.

wharf n wharf: dock, pier
They dangled their legs off the *wharf* into the water below.

wheedle v whee-dle: to coax, persuade
She *wheedled* her kitten to come down out of the tree.

wheeze v wheeze: to breathe with difficulty
They *wheezed* in the dust that flew around them.

wheeze n wheeze: a wheezing
From the sound of that *wheeze*, I suspect that you are getting a cold.

whet v whet: to sharpen
Whet the knife against this rock.

whiff n whiff: slight smell
A *whiff* of flowers could be detected in the air.

whiff v whiff: to blow or puff
The bubbles *whiffed* lightly across the lawn.

whimper n whim-per: low, mournful sound
A *whimper* could be heard from the hospital room.

whimper v whim-per: to cry or utter with complaint
She *whimpered* at the disappearance of her puppy.

whine v whine: to cry complainingly
She *whined* to her father when her brother broke her doll.

whine n whine: a complaint uttered in a whining tone
A baby's *whine* is hard to ignore.

whirl v whirl: to spin, rotate quickly
The falling leaves *whirled* in the air before settling on the ground.

whisk v whisk: to sweep, brush
He *whisked* the papers under the desk top.
whisk n whisk: quick movement
A *whisk* of wind sent the seeds flying over the land.
wield v wield: to hold and use, control
He *wielded* a paintbrush in his left hand as he studied the painting.
wilt v wilt: to droop
By the tenth lap around the lake, they were *wilting* from all the exercising.
wily adj wi-ly: crafty, sly
He was *wily* enough to get away with the forgery.
wince v wince: to shrink from
He *winced* from her verbal abuse.
windfall n wind-fall: unexpected good luck
They were delighted to receive a *windfall* of an inheritance.
wisp n wisp: small bunch
A *wisp* of hair escaped from under her scarf.
wistful adj wist-ful: yearning
She gazed upon her idol with a *wistful* desire to be closer.
wither v with-er: to dry up, to cause to wither
The flowers *withered* under the hot sun.
witty adj wit-ty: clever and amusing
Her *witty* remarks entertained the other diners.
woe n woe: great grief, trouble
His friends tried to lighten his *woe* when he lost his job.
wrangle v wran-gle: to quarrel angrily
The squirrels *wrangled* over the morsels in the box.
wrath n wrath: rage, anger
She reacted to their insults with extreme *wrath*.
wrest v wrest: to pull, twist
They tried in vain to *wrest* the bone away from their dog.
wretch n wretch: bad person
He is considered to be such a *wretch* that no one visits him.
wring v wring: to squeeze
Wring the water out of that towel before you hand it to me.
writhe v writhe: to twist
He *writhed* in pain from the impact of the board on his back.
writhe n writhe: a writhing
A *writhe* of pain resulted when she pulled too hard.
wry adj wry: twisted
His *wry* sense of humor sometimes gets him into trouble with people.

X, Y, Z

xylophone n xy-lo-phone: musical instrument
He plays a *xylophone* in the orchestra.

yam n yam: sweet potato
His favorite vegetables are *yams* served with butter and brown sugar.

yearn v yearn: to desire, long for
She *yearned* for the days when all her children were still at home.

yelp v yelp: to utter a short cry
The kids *yelped* when they first plunged into the cold water.

yelp n yelp: quick, sharp cry
A *yelp* escaped from his mouth when he backed into the hot radiator.

yield v yield: to produce, give
The crop *yielded* a large amount of vegetables.

yield n yield: the amount yielded or produced
Their *yield* far exceeded their expectations.

yoke n yoke: wooden frame
The *yoke* around the oxen's neck was painted a bright color.

yoke v yoke: to harness
Yoke the horse before you attempt to ride him.

zany n za-ny: silly person
That clown is such a *zany* that all the children enjoy him.

zany adj za-ny: of or like a zany, foolish
His *zany* antics kept the audience laughing.

zeal n zeal: enthusiasm, desire
Her *zeal* was contagious as we all joined in to complete the job.

zenith n ze-nith: highest point
He reached the *zenith* of his career when he was appointed chairman of the company.

zephyr n zeph-yr: gentle wind, breeze
A *zephyr* from the ocean cooled their bodies.

zeppelin n zep-pe-lin: dirigible, blimp
The highlight of the state fair was the ride in the *zeppelin* over the city.

zest n zest: enjoyment, exciting quality
Her *zest* for her work is noticeable.

zither n zith-er: musical instrument
He can play everything from piano to *zither* to violin.

zoology n zo-ol-o-gy: science of animals
His upbringing on a farm certainly helped him with his study of *zoology*.